Dedication

To my Hazel for her patience
and continuous encouragement

Sofia's Story

Life In Cracow

She woke early. It was hot in their small flat in Cracow. Despite Tomas' warnings about burglars, she'd left the bedroom and hall window open some nights. But even that didn't help on still, windless evenings like this.

Her body glistened with sweat as she stared aimlessly at the ceiling. She and Tomas had been married three years now and sex had become a routine event, usually fueled by a night of binge drinking on his part. She felt as if she'd become a rubber doll.

Tomas rarely had trouble sleeping due to his nightly alcohol intake and, unlike in the early days of their marriage, he rarely woke up with an erection that she could mount and ride until she came.

She thought about going to the bathroom to splash cold water on her face, neck and breasts, in the hope that feeling cooler, even temporarily, might help her drift back off to sleep. Instead she lay there, watching the ceiling fan spin round and round in the hope that she'd find peace.

Tonight was more difficult however as she had a lot on her mind. Tomorrow after she had finished work, she would sit her exam at the School For English Language. She'd been going there for an hour and a half every Wednesday evening for two years and passing her final Diploma would help her to get a better job; perhaps at the front desk in a hotel or even in a bank. Increasingly however her thoughts were of escape.

Last year, her improved English language skills had enabled her to change her job as a laundry worker to become a waitress in a city centre restaurant. Sofia loved her job, even though the hours were long. She was usually tired when she returned home after being on her feet all day. However, she could observe the daily hustle and bustle of life in a cosmopolitan city.

Tables turned continuously and there were all kinds of actors in her theatre; well-dressed businessmen having working breakfasts, lunches and dinners; friends talking excitedly as they sipped their cappuccinos and lattes; lonely men and women, trying to pass the time as voyeurs of city life. But most of all, Sofia liked to watch the lovers, all ages and most happy say little as they held hands and gazed into each other's eyes.

She looked across the bed to where Tomas lay face down, the sound of his irregular low snore demonstrating the fact that he was in a deep sleep. They had been together for six years, married for three. At first she liked the fact that he was big and strong and that he took her clubbing on Friday and Saturday nights where they danced for hours.

He had wanted her, she knew that as he often took her up alleys on the way home and thrust himself into her, and sometimes he bent her over and entered her from behind, making her gasp as he almost split her in half.

Now however, they hardly went out together. They were supposed to be saving to rent a bigger home and have a family, but most of his spare money went on drink, and she made sure that there was no chance of what would have been an unwanted pregnancy on her part. She increasingly thought that there seemed to be little point in continuing as they were. All she seemed to do was cook and clear up after him. Conversation had never been brilliant between them and was virtually non-existent now.

The alarm rang at five thirty. Tomas groaned and climbed slowly out of bed. No early morning kiss, just the non-romantic sounds of his early morning ablutions from the bathroom next door. Ten minutes later, after a hurried black coffee, he was out of the front door and on his way to the railway depot where he worked. He stopped to shout up the stairs to tell her to have his dinner ready in the oven as he would be going out to the Workers Social Club at eight and would not be back until late. There were no good luck wishes for her exam.

She rose at seven, even though there was no need as she had taken the day off work. However, she'd promised her mother and sister that she would call in and see them today. One hour later, after a tram and bus ride, she was knocking on the door of her mother's flat, on the third floor of a city estate block.

Her sister had moved back in to care for their mother, who had been in poor health since the death of Sofia's father from a heart attack almost two years ago. Sofia's sister was twenty-nine, unmarried, overweight and worked part time in a bakery. Not good for her mother who was living on a comfort food diet of pies and cream cakes.

It had been two weeks since Sofia's last visit. The door opened and her elder sister Agnieska kissed her on the cheek.

'Come in. Mother has cooked breakfast for you.' Agnieska turned inwards and Sofia followed.

In her early twenties Agnieszka had a brief relationship with an older man. Since then she appeared to have given up on the opposite sex, settling instead into a life of endless television and occasional family meetings. Like her mother's, her weight had ballooned.

'Good morning Mama, how are you? You look well,' lied Sofia.

'All the better for seeing you daughter. You look thinner and thinner every time I see you. I'm sure you never eat. You're too busy running around after that no good husband of yours. Sit down and I'll put a proper breakfast in front of you.'

Sofia sat down to confront a plateful of greasy sausages and two eggs sunny side up, with two bread doorsteps on each side. Just as well she was not pregnant as she would not have been able to keep it down.

Half an hour later she'd eaten enough to satisfy her watchful mother. As usual on such visits, while she ate, her mother and sister picked over the details of her life. How was work? Had she seen any celebrities? Were there any scandals? Was she pregnant yet? Tomas must be a useless lover, declared her mother, a good catholic. She would have disowned Sofia if she knew she'd been practicing birth control for three years.

'How long will your exam take? When will you know the result?' asked Agnieszka.

'One and a half hours. I'll get a letter telling me the result in a month's time. Why don't you enroll Agnieszka? You were cleverer than me at school.'

'I'm far too busy looking after mama to waste one evening a week going back to school. I don't need to speak English in my job.'

Her mother nodded in support. She would be terrified of living alone.

At midday Sofia announced her departure, She would go and sit outside her restaurant and revise before the exam which began at half past four.

She got there just after one, ordered a discounted Americano and a free glass of water, and opened the first of her course files.

She'd been sitting for thirty minutes when there was a tap on her shoulder. She turned to see Harris, an American student who had been working at the cafe for the past three months. He was of Polish descent and fitted in well as one of the restaurant team. 'Would you like me to help you for half an hour, before my shift starts?'

'That would help me a lot. OK. I'll try and translate this Polish novel extract into English. Don't hesitate to correct me.'

Thirty minutes flew by and she thanked Harris for his help. When they were on shift together their glances often met, and she wondered if he wanted to ask her out, though if he did, he had not yet summoned up the courage. Had he done so, the answer would have been yes.

At twenty five past four, the exam papers were handed out and the fourteen students, eleven of whom were women, were given five minutes to read the questions before a buzzer told them it was time to begin. The exam comprised of three sections: A Polish to English translation, an English tract to translate into Polish, and a series of English paragraphs to punctuate.

The next one and a half hours passed quickly until the buzzer sounded again and Sofia thought she'd done well, although she'd found the punctuation difficult. The thirty minutes spent with Harris had been beneficial and it had done her confidence good to see four of the students walk out within the first thirty minutes.

She'd planned to go straight home after the exam, but a few of the students wanted to go for a drink to discuss the questions, so she thought she might as well join them, rather than be alone in the flat yet again.

One drink turned into two, then three, and it was after eleven when she finally returned home. She knew something was wrong when she smelt the aroma of burnt food. Tomas launched into her as soon as she walked into the flat. 'Where have you been, you slut? I give up my night to cook you a meal and you stay out drinking and whoring!'

There were empty beer bottles scattered all over the kitchen and she could smell the alcohol on his breath. He grabbed her and threw her roughly onto the kitchen table.

'What have you got to say for yourself, bitch? I checked with your college and your exam finished at six. What have you been doing for the last five hours? How many students and teachers have you fucked?'

Sofia opened her mouth to reply but before she could utter a word Tomas slapped her hard across the face. Her head was spinning.

'I'll show you what whores get!'

He tore off her jeans and underwear and turned her face down on the tabletop. Sofia struggled but was helpless against his violent rage. He held her down with his hands around her throat and rammed her dry anus time after time. She screamed for him to get of, but her cries did nothing to stem his attack.

Tears flooded her cheeks. She could feel the bruising on her neck when he finally climbed off her, lurched into the bedroom and collapsed across the bed.

For the next few days there was an embarrassed silence between them. She could sense that he wanted to apologize, but he could not overcome his shame.

For her part, she kept out of his way. She slept in the living room and did not visit her mother until the bruising could be sufficiently hidden by make-up.

When she finally did visit, after the usual mixture of food and gossip, she took the opportunity to say to Agnieszka 'Don't worry if you don't hear from me for a while. Tomas and I had a dreadful fight. I'm thinking of moving away and I don't want him to know where I am.'

'I don't blame you for leaving that pig, but don't take too before you get in touch as we'll worry about you. For now, I won't say anything to mama. If she asks I'll tell her you're busy at work. And when you go, don't give me the address, at least, not at first. That way Tomas won't be able to get anything out of me.'

But weeks passed, then months, without Sofia making a definite resolve, though she continued to sleep in the living room. Then, one day on her way to work, she noticed that someone had left a newspaper behind so she picked it up. After reading the national and local news, her attention was grabbed by a quarter page advertisement.

FRONTIER RECRUITMENT AGENCY

Hotel reception and office/shop work in England, Scotland and Ireland for applicants with a good level of written and spoken English. Excellent rates of pay. Applicants must have a European Passport.

When she got off the tram Sofia took the paper with her and thought about the advert for the whole morning, until she summoned up the courage to call the agency and arrange an appointment for the following Wednesday morning. The receptionist sounded extremely professional and Sofia noted the request that she should bring her passport along with her for verification.

Towards the end of the shift, Harris came up to her and asked if she was OK. Sofia asked him if he had time for a coffee after work, as she wanted his input on an important decision she was about to make. He readily agreed.

They went to the nearest Costa where Harris insisted on buying the coffees. When he set the cups on the table and sat down, he told Sofia that he'd be leaving at the end of the month.

'What can I say? Itchy feet.' He said. 'The whole purpose of this trip is to see as much of Europe as possible. I've been here too long already.'

'I'm so sorry!' exclaimed Sofia 'I feel as if I'm losing my only true friend.

She went on to unburden her feelings and told Harris that she was thinking of running away to England.

'Come travelling with me.' Harris looked straight into her eyes and she felt herself go weak at the knees.

'Where are you going next?' Sofia was desperately trying to get her head around what Harris had asked.

'I have three months left on my visa, and I've saved up enough money to go touring around the Croatian Islands and Italy before I go back to the states'

'That sounds wonderful. Let me think about it and maybe we can meet and talk again in more detail.'

'Does this mean that you're giving up on your marriage?' said Harris.

'My marriage is dead,' said Sofia, the words leaving her mouth before she had time to consider what she was saying.

Harris' flight to Croatia left in fourteen days, so he and Sofia agreed to meet for dinner after a week and come to a decision. The next seven days flew by and still Sofia had not spoken at all to Tomas. In her mind she was sure that her marriage was over.

When the appointed time came, Sofia spent an extra thirty minutes in the bathroom, applying make-up and brushing her hair until it shone. She put on her sexiest underwear and applied her most expensive perfume in the places that she would want to be kissed.

Harris had booked a table at a cosy Italian trattoria. After work they went straight there and Harris ordered the first of several bottles of Chianti. He started by walking her through his itinerary. She was spellbound by his description of the

Croatian Islands and made no move to remove his hand when he gently placed it over hers. His fingers were warm and strong and she felt the heat percolating through her body, aided by the inner glow from the Chianti.

At eleven thirty she looked around and realised that they were the only customers left. Harris asked her if she would come back to his flat, and they left the restaurant hand-in-hand.

Harris' duplex was a short walk away down quiet streets. He opened the door, ushered Sofia inside, and before they had taken three steps into the room they were kissing frantically.

She was a little shy as he undressed her and carried her into the bedroom, but soon lost her inhibitions as his fingers entered her, slowly prising open her vagina.

Sofia caressed his hair, before digging her nails into his back as her body arched in response to his flickering tongue.

The hours passed as she drifted in and out of ecstasy. She had never felt like this before. Eventually she and Harris tell asleep entwined in each other's arms.

The alarm clock jolted them awake at six. After a lingering fifteen minutes in the shower together, Harris took his leave of her, telling her that he would come and meet her at work at the end of his shift.

Remembering her appointment with the employment agency, Sofia dressed quickly. Her first thoughts were to call and cancel as she wanted to travel with Harris, but she reasoned that she should not pass up an opportunity that might have an important bearing on her life.

Reason won the day and she caught the early morning tram back to her apartment.

Her heart sank as she saw the refuse bags piled up on the landing outside the door. Sure enough they contained her clothes, stuffed inside and overflowing. She went to open the door and discovered that her key no longer worked. After hammering on the woodwork and shouting Tomas' name, she noticed a piece of paper protruding from underneath the doormat and she reached down to it. She did not need spectacles to assimilate the message.

Fuck off whore!!

She slumped on the top step and leaned against the bannister, gathering her thoughts; glad she'd put her passport in her bag the previous day to avoid forgetting it.

She decided to take her clothes to her mother's and travel from there to the interview. She would decide what to do next when she met Harris early that evening.

The Snatch

Sofia arrived for her interview in good time. She went to Reception, which was on the ground floor, and introduced herself to the receptionist, to be told that the interview panel would convene in five minutes.

She picked up a fashion magazine from the coffee table in front of her and browsed through the contents.

Sure enough, after five minutes the door opened and a large, well-dressed man asked her to follow him. He led her along a corridor to a room adjacent to some stairs going down to the basement.

Inside two men and a woman were sat around a circular table. There was an empty chair near the door, into which Sofia was ushered.

The room was light and airy and the walls were hung with photographs of hotel lobbies and smart office interiors. Sofia relaxed. After all, this was only one her possible options. If she didn't get the job, so what? She'd leave for Croatia with Harris instead.

The large man pulled up a chair spoke and introduced himself as Mr. Borzinsky, Managing Director of Frontier. His colleagues followed suit. Miss Kalowski and Mr. Smyslov. All spoke with distinct Russian accents.

Borzinsky explained that there would be two interviews; the first to establish her qualifications and suitability for the positions that they were aiming to fill at the moment. Should she satisfy those requirements there would be a second interview in a week's time, at which they would present her with a range options.

He started by asking her to describe her family and marital situations. She mentioned about her mother and her sister and then said she had recently separated from her husband. The interviewers exchanged glances

Borizov said that he needed to ask her some questions about her work history, but first there'd be a coffee break.

While they were waiting for the drinks to arrive, Miss Kalowski asked Sofia about her physical characteristics: height, weight, and whether she coloured her hair, before checking if she had any preferences about where she would like to work.

' I'd prefer the United Kingdom, but I'd also be prepared to work on a cruise ship.'

' What about France?'

'I studied French at school but I haven't had any real opportunity to develop my language skills since I left.'

A knock on the door announced the arrival of the receptionist with a tray of drinks, which she served to those seated at the table.

Borizov enquired if Sofia had her passport with her and when she confirmed that she did, he asked if she'd mind if they photocopied it to save her bringing to the second interview, should she be called for one.

'It will only take a moment, and if you're not successful we'll destroy the copies, so there's no danger to you. So, if you're happy, Miss Kalowski will see to it now.'

Sofia nodded and handed over the document. By now she'd drunk over half her coffee. Borizov asked her how long she had been at her current job. She tried to answer but her mind felt clouded and her tongue refused to form the words she wanted to say.

The room began to spin and Sofia made a mumbled request for a glass of water before darkness descended.

When she came to she was lying on a bed in a darkened room, fully clothed. She tried to get up but couldn't as her hands and ankles were manacled to the bed frame.

She was still feeling woozy but the adrenaline surge racing through body soon cleared any last trace of grogginess from her mind. She called for help until her throat was raw from yelling, but no one came, and she guessed the room was probably soundproofed. Eventually exhaustion trumped blind panic and she drifted off into a deep sleep.

The next thing she knew, she was being violently shaken. She opened her eyes. The lights were on now and Borizov and Smyslov stood beside the bed, no longer dressed in suits but jeans and tee shirts.

'You must be thirsty.' said Borizov and held a bottle of water to her lips. Her thirst overcame her fear that it was drugged and she drank greedily until Borizov pulled the bottle away.

'Where am I? What day is it?'

'Time has no meaning for you any more babushka.' said Borizov, with a slow smile on his face. He reached out and stroked her hair.

'Good news. You passed the interview. Well done. Now you are my slave. If you're good and do as you're told you can look forward to being free in a few years time. But if you don't behave…'

The threat hung in the air until with one quick movement he ripped open her blouse, eased her right nipple out of her bra and bit down hard. She screamed. Smyslov grinned and licked his lips.

'I supply girls to brothels all over France, Holland, Belgium and Germany. Watch the television in the corner.'

Smyslov went over and turned on the TV, inserting a DVD into the drive. After an introductory screen entitled *Frontier Training Video* there were stock shots of leafy streets on a city that could have been anywhere in Europe.

A well-dressed Arab walked a pavement and turned toward a ground floor flat with a bright red door where he rang the bell. After a few seconds the door opened and a voluptuous blond woman in a negligee stood there smiling.

In the next scene the same woman, naked now and on all fours on a luxurious bed, was being violently serviced by the Arab man with an accompanying sound track of moans and grunts.

When he finished, the Arab handed over a large bunch of notes and said he would recommend the woman to some of his friends, suggesting several of them could get together for some fun one evening. The woman gave him a sexy smile and said 'No problem, though of course it will cost extra if we film it all.'

Then the action shifted to a large house in a city suburb, were eight young women sat on three sofas, naked apart from a pair of briefs. An old woman escorted an elderly man into the room and introduced the women, telling him what sex acts each of them specialised in.

Then the film cut to a bedroom where one of the girls gave the man a blowjob while he reclined in an armchair.

The DVD ended with a visit to a seedy property close to a busy docks area. The cameraman entered a room off a gloomy corridor, where a naked woman was tied to a bed. She was hollow eyed and her torso and breasts were covered in bruises.

A man knelt beside her. He held a syringe and inserted the needle into a vein on her arm. She gave a low moan but there was no movement from her. Another man entered the room. He slapped the woman's face before flipping her over and raping her.

'What do you think of our training video?' asked Borizov. 'There are three possible futures for you. If you're cooperative and let Peter and I spend some time with you on film, we'll give you work in one of our brothels. If you show talent there we'll set you up as a top of the range call girl. This is a good option as you get to keep ten percent of your earnings. Who knows? After two or three years you might have earned enough to buy back your passport, and if you're really lucky or you could meet a wealthy client who'll do this for you.

Otherwise, we expect you work in the brothel for five years and continue to please your clients. At the end of that time we'll consider letting you go, if your family can pay for your release that is.

And then there's option three. If you cause me trouble at any time, you'll spend the rest of your days chained to a bed in the docklands until you die from an STD or heroin overdose.

I'll you now for a few hours to think over your choices, and as you've been a good girl today, I'll send in some food and water.'

After the men left, Sofia sobbed for a while. She thought about the dinner date she wouldn't make with Harris and imagined his disappointment when she didn't show up. Perhaps he was already looking for her.

Eventually, she did some cold hard reasoning. There seemed little possibility of escape and a high risk of death or injury if she tried. The thought of becoming a prostitute repulsed her but she'd lost her virginity some time ago and sex with Tomas quite often felt unemotional. She often just lay there, waiting for it to end.

The Oldest Profession

By the time Borizov and Smyslov returned Sofia had resolved to obey them. 'Did you enjoy your meal?' asked Borizov and she nodded.

'The last meal of the condemned.' she said.

'There's no need to feel like that. Peter and I are experienced actors and we can help you to realise your potential. We have a cameraman in the next room filming everything so this is your chance to win an Oscar!'

Smyslov undid the manacles on the bed and told her he would take her to have a shower if she would first remove her clothes. He looked at her appreciatively when she complied.

On her return they gave her various instructions, asking her to pose this ay and that before the camera. Borizov then came and stood behind her. He held a bottle of olive oil and proceeded to massage her breasts with it, rubbing it in slowly.

Meanwhile, Smyslov took his clothes off and knelt before her. She gasped as he inserted his fingers into her vagina and began to massage her clitoris.

By this time, her nipples were erect. When Smyslov began to work on her with his tongue, she could feel herself moisten and she began to make noises as he worked her faster and faster.

She could feel her juice running down her thighs. Smyslov got up and came and stood in front of her while Borizov, naked now, came and stood behind her.

Smyslov bent her forward and inserted his penis into her mouth. 'Swallow me you Polish bitch!'

She gagged at first but she had performed oral sex many times with Tomas and soon had the Russian groaning with pleasure.

While she was doing this she felt Borizov's hand working her vagina. She guessed what was coming next and was apprehensive as his penis was huge, much bigger than either Tomas' or Harris'. She was relieved when he inserted some lubricant first before slowly penetrating her.

Sofia gasped as she felt him probe deep inside her. It did not seem long until all three of them came in a cacophony of loud exclamations.

After a brief interlude during which they all rested and drank vodka, they resumed activities, this time with her astride Smyslov while giving Borizov oral succor.

After they had all climaxed once more, the men got dressed. 'You're a natural Sofia,' said Borizov. 'Your husband was a very lucky man. One more thing, if you ever try to escape from me, your mother and sister will receive a copy of these tapes and I will send one to your boyfriend too, if we can find him.'

Until now Sofia had managed to keep her mind blank, but Borizov's words resulted in shame flooding over her and once she was alone she sobbed herself to sleep.

Over the next week, the video scene was repeated many times, with a cast of different actors. One day she was given a vibrator and filmed while she used it on her breasts, vagina and anus.

At least the food was good. Each evening Sofia found that she had a ravenous appetite. There was even a glass of red wine with dinner.

One morning Sofia awoke in a panic. She was manacled to a bed again and a gag had been inserted in her mouth. It was completely dark but as her eyes became accustomed to the gloom she could make out the shape of four other beds. She realised she was in the back of a lorry. She could hear its engine, particularly as it travelled uphill.

After what seemed like an age, the lorry stopped and she heard the door being pushed up. Light flooded the container and two men with shaved heads climbed in.

Sofia could now see there were other women chained, one to each bed. All of them blinked against the bright sunlight. Two of the women had large bruises on their cheeks and one had a gash on her ear that, from the look of it, had only recently stopped bleeding.

Sofia succeeded in raising herself slightly so that she could see out of the back of the lorry. They were in a hilly/mountainous area and she could see no sign of civilization or any other traffic.

'Right, who wants feeding?' said the bigger of the men in English with a thick Eastern European accent. He opened a carrier bag and pulled out some bread, cheese and several bottles of water.

The women nodded their heads.

'That's good.' said the man, with a leer spreading across his face. 'But there is no such thing as a free lunch!'

He nodded to his colleague and they went to each of the beds in turn and pulled up the women's tops and exposed their breasts, then slid up their skirts and pulled down their panties.

'Take your pick! I'm going to help myself to some of this ginger cunt. I reckon it's begging for my cock.' said the leader, as he walked to the bed opposite to Sofia. The other man walked towards the bed on where the youngest woman lay. She looked no older than sixteen at the most.

Both men took off their trousers. The boss began to lick the girl's nipples and before sliding his fingers into her. Sofia could hear her moan behind the gag and watched the tears roll down her cheeks as the man climbed onto her and began to thrust in her faster and faster.

After both men had finished, the men undid the women's gags and fed them some cheese and bread and gave them a bottle of water, which they gulped down hungrily.

'There is another bottle of water for you if you turn over and let us give it to you up your arse.' said the talkative one.

Sofia's neighbor remained completely still but with vacant eyes the young girl slowly turned over, and after what seemed like another half an hour of continuous grunting with occasional exclamations, both men had had their fill.

The leader came and sat on Sofia's bed ' I bet you thought you'd escaped all of that fun.' He said, as he put his hand into the bag and pulled out a packet of Viagra tablets. He smiled, took three and handed three to his colleague.

Then he untied Sofia's gag and fed her some cheese and gave her some water. He turned to Sofia and leered ' Well. I guess I am ready for action again.'

Sofia steeled herself as he stroked and bit down on her nipples. She turned her head to the side in order to avoid the stench of his bad breath. Then, she gasped as she felt him penetrate her. He took longer than he had with his first victim due to the effects of the Viagra but eventually he slowed and then withdrew.

'Ok, who wants another bottle of water?' Neither Sofia nor the woman on the next bed moved.
'Well, I'm not going to waste three Viagra tablets,' said the man as he tried to turn Sofia over. She steeled her body and resisted but received a violent slap across her face for her trouble.

The next fifteen minutes were sheer agony as she was sodomised. Tears ran down her face. The girl in the next bed mouthed that it would soon be over.

Afterwards, the men got dressed. The one Sofia thought of as the leader told the women that they were only half way on their journey and they would each have to take another pill to knock them out until they reached their destination.

Life In The Birdcage

When Sofia next woke up the first thing she noticed was that she was not restrained. She lay on one of two three-quarter beds in a large room, furnished with wardrobes, a sofa and two chests of drawers.

The curtains were closed. Eventually Sofia felt steady enough to get off the bed and walk to the window. She pulled the curtains back and light flooded into the room causing her to squint. It felt like days since she had seen sunlight.

Outside she saw a rectangular, lawned garden, surrounded by fields that stretched for miles. Several cars were parked at the front of the house and a single-track road ran ramrod straight into the distance.

Sofia slumped back onto the bed and was about to nod off to sleep again when the door opened and a tall, willowy brunette entered. She had on a short dress that barely covered her thighs. Her large breasts spilled over the flimsy neckline. 'Ah, sleeping beauty has woken.' she smiled.

Sofia couldn't help but stare at the newcomer. She was beautiful and had an amazing figure, though her sunken, lifeless eyes spoiled her glamorous image. 'Welcome to Hollywood. I'm Jana.' said the woman in Polish.

Sofia introduced herself and asked 'Where am I?'

'Somewhere in France. None of us know where exactly. Madame Lafarge will be coming to fetch you soon.' And with that, Jana left the room.

Sofia's curiosity got the better of her and she opened the wardrobes and drawers to discover a large number of dresses like Jana had worn in a wide range of colours, plus dressing gowns and flimsy underwear. Several pairs of high-heeled shoes and sandals filled the bottom of each wardrobe.

Sofia started as the door opened again and a well-dressed woman with immaculate hair entered the room, followed by a huge brute of a man who looked totally evil.

'I see you are making yourself at home,' said the woman. 'Just as well as this will be your room for the foreseeable future. I will give you a tour of the building with the other new arrivals after dinner. My name is Madame Lafarge and this is my establishment. I have a business arrangement with Monsieur Borizov. Get yourself freshened up and put on one of the dresses and a pair of shoes from the wardrobe on the right. They will all fit. You were measured when you were asleep in Cracow. There's a range of make up and perfumes in the top drawer of the chest on the right. Igor will come for you in one hour.'

And with that, Madame Lafarge and the man Sofia assumed was Igor left the room.

Sofia spent the next half hour choosing her outfit and applying make up. She was putting the finishing touches to her bright red lipstick when Jana returned.
'Ah. You're going on the beauty parade. Make the most of this one. It is the only one you attend here that is not followed by hours of groping and penetration.'

'How long have you been here?' Sofia asked her roommate.

'About a year,' said Jana. 'I had my own apartment in Paris but two of my clients complained that I needed drugs to perform to their requirements so I was brought back here.'

It was then that Sofia noticed the track marks on Jana's arms. 'Did you not save up enough to buy your freedom?' she asked.

Jana laughed. 'I was in Paris for two years, but nearly all of my earnings went on paying for the apartment and drugs. When I first moved there, one of my clients told me he loved me and that we would move in together. But, when he told his parents about me, he was spirited off to St Kitts and never returned.

I realized that my time was limited when they began using me more and more for parties, which were usually paid for by a wealthy Arab. A few girls would be subjected to sustained sexual assault by a large group of men. Everything was filmed and played back later for the Arab's amusement.'

The door opened. Igor stood there. 'Follow me.' he uttered and led the way to the ground floor, down a large winding staircase.

Sofia noted that they were in a broad entrance hall and that the front door was closed. A man sat at a desk, his fingers pecking away at a computer keyboard. A second man stood beside the door. Both wore dinner jackets.

Igor escorted Sofia into a large, elegantly furnished salon. Her three travelling companions were already there, along with Madame Lafarge and four other women. All of them wore dresses similar to Sofia's. They held glasses of what looked like champagne.

'Welcome Sofia.' said Madame Lafarge. 'Let me introduce you to your new colleagues. From left to right we you're Magda, Elena and Helena who you met on the journey. Then we have Irena, another Elena, Lara and Suki, who have worked here for some time. I'll leave you to get to know each other and will join you for dinner in fifteen minutes, after which I will be your guide on a tour of the house.'

The new arrivals congregated together and asked each other where they had come from. Sofia's neighbor on the lorry ordeal was Elena. She was Ukrainian but spoke some Polish along with fairly good English. She worked in an office in Kiev until she answered a Frontier advertisement. The youngest girl, Magda, was Polish, also from Cracow. She'd been clubbing with some friends when she passed out after having a vodka and coke. The next thing she remembered was waking up manacled to a bed, in the basement of an unfamiliar house.

Magda had undergone the same induction as Sofia. She did not have a passport but had her identity card had been enough and she was taken. Helena worked as a barmaid in Warsaw and had also been abducted during a night out. Her family lived in a village in the country and she had not been in touch with them for some years, as she'd run away from home to avoid continuing abuse by her father.

The four new girls plied the older residents with questions, mostly about what they would be expected to do. It would have been easier to ask what they were *not* expected to do. Twosomes, threesomes, plus upward, oral, vaginal and anal sex were standard. Lesbian shows were popular too and Madame Lafarge would give them some training in that area.

It turned out that Suki was the resident dominatrix,

Originally from Thailand, she came to Paris and had worked

in the vice industry since she was sixteen.

Igor reappeared and told them to follow him to the dining

room, another elegantly furnished chamber where crystal

glassware shimmered on the table.

After they were seated, Madame Lafarge explained that

some of the guests paid an inclusive fee for dinner with a

chosen partner, followed by sexual entertainment. Other

guests selected an escort for the evening and were shown

directly to a room.

After the meal and a cup of coffee, Madame Lafarge told the

girls to follow her for the tour, which began upstairs where

there were twelve rooms, all tastefully furnished with large beds, some of which were four-posters. Sofia could not help but notice the stands in each room, which contained various whips, handcuffs, ropes and a selection of vibrators. Condoms and lubricants were laid ready on the bedside tables. There were several shower rooms and bathrooms too.

When they returned to the lower floor they were shown two of the four remaining rooms, the Lesbian filming room and the Bondage dungeon. Madame Lafarge informed them that she lived in the cottage adjacent to the house.

The lesbian room had two or three beds and sofas, set at different angles. All the ceilings were mirrored and cameras were positioned around each room to maximize the view.

In the Bondage room Suki stepped out of her evening dress and donned a leather outfit, which had distinct echoes of

Barbarella. She put on a black helmet with a grill, picked up a whip and snapped it loudly. The girls started which brought a sneer to Suki's face. 'This is the room of pain,' she said slowly and began to point to various cages, dog leads and manacles that were spread around the room. 'Over the next few weeks, you will all come to watch me entertain my clients and then each of you will try out being a dominatrix to see if you like it.'

Once the tour was over they gathered in the hallway. 'Are there any questions?' said Madame Lafarge.

Helena put up her hand shyly 'Excuse me, but what happens if any of our clients become violent?'

'There is closed circuit TV in all of the rooms, and the doorman and his assistant can monitor everything that goes on. They will intervene if they think that any of you are in real danger. However the odd bruise or two goes with the nature of the work.

So, that's it for this evening girls. Make sure you get your beauty sleep. You will be at work from one pm tomorrow until two o'clock the following morning. This will be your daily routine for six days a week. On the seventh day you can rest and enjoy the grounds, and occasionally we will have a supervised shopping outing. There is a kitchen, next to the bondage room, where you will eat all of your meals, unless you are invited to the guest's dining room. And don't worry. You will not be put off your food by the screams. The bondage room is sound proofed!

And one final warning. Mr. Borizov told you all the penalty for trying to escape. I will repeat it. If caught during or after an escape, you will be held and tortured for a week in the bondage room. Then you will be shipped to one of our Docklands hotels.'

On that somber note, the women wound their way up the stairs to bed.

Sofia slept better than she had done for some time. Perhaps it was the wine she had drunk the previous night.

She dressed and went down to find some breakfast. Magda and Elena were already in the small kitchen when she appeared. They all spoke English as best as they could.

Sofia asked if either of them spoke any French, but neither knew any more than a few elementary words. Sofia said she would ask Madame Lafarge if they could have lessons. It would help to pass the time. They all agreed that what was about to happen in their lives was an improvement on the past month.

After breakfast they went for a walk in the grounds, closely followed by one of the armed security men. They returned to the kitchen and were having coffee when Madame Lafarge entered and told them to go to their rooms and get ready for work. They were told to come down to the reception room wearing high-heeled shoes, panties and nothing else.

Sofia was one of the last to arrive. She blushed as she took her place beside the other girls on the sofas. An empty sofa stood opposite them.

Sofia noticed that nearly all of the girls had tattoos, mostly on the base of their spines. She and Elena were the only two women not to have any ink on their skin. Magda was covered in blue-green artwork. Several girls had studs in their nose and one or two had pierced tongues.

Madame Lafarge entered and told them the first customers would be admitted in fifteen minutes. 'Do all of you know how to perform oral and anal sex?' The girls all nodded their heads.

'Good. I will be watching you all on the CCTV television this week. If any of you are not performing as I expect, I will tell you and see that you are given some education, and if that doesn't have the desired effect you will be taken to the docklands. If any of you display special talents, I will add you to the waiting list for Paris. However, we must be able to trust you absolutely for that to happen.'

Soon there was a knock on the door and two men were admitted, both overweight and in their forties.

Madame Lafarge introduced the girls and quoted an hourly rate. The fees varied and Sofia was surprised to note that other than Suki, she was the joint highest with Magda, at fifteen hundred francs. Three of the older girls who had been here some time were priced at seven hundred and fifty francs per hour. The men were told that if they wished to spend some time in the Bondage room that it was two and a half thousand francs per hour.

Both of the men selected girls at the cheaper rate and were led upstairs. Sofia and Magda were next to be chosen when a group of four men arrived. They fondled the girls and made remarks to each other in French before making their choice. Sofia's partner looked to be in his mid-thirties. He was unshaven but good looking in a rugged kind of way.

Once they were in a bedroom, Sofia tried to make conversation in halting French, but the man smiled and said

'Don't worry Cherie. I speak some English, Where are you from?'

Sofia told him she was from Cracow 'Ah.' he replied, 'It will be interesting to see if you come in English or Polish.'

He smiled at her. 'My name is Pierre. You can call my cock whatever you like!'

Pierre undressed and lay on the bed. He beckoned Sofia to him and she began by giving him oral sex. When he was close to ejaculation she eased off and climbed astride him. It did not take long for him to achieve the first of several ejaculations and she feigned reciprocation on three occasions; once in Polish, once in French and once in English, just to make sure.

Eventually they both drifted off to sleep and when Pierre woke her it was after six o' clock. After one more for the road they returned to the reception room where Pierre paid his bill and stuffed a thousand franc note down the front of her panties. A kiss and he was gone, saying 'I will return the next time we dock in Marseilles.'

Southern France then. That explained the hot temperatures when they left the house. Madame Lafarge made certain that they all wore sunscreen when they walked in the grounds.

Sofia asked Madame Lafarge if she could have a shower, which was approved. She washed quickly, returned to duty, and was selected on two further occasions that night, both for one hour by elderly gentlemen who required some assistance before performing full sex.

Sofia lay awake after she returned to bed wanting to compare notes with Jana, but her roommate did not arrive and in the morning Sofia discovered that Jana had spent the night at a 'party' in Marseilles. Alone again, Sofia thought of her mother and sister. They must be so worried about her.

But Madame Lafarge had made it clear that the girls were not allowed to phone their families or former boyfriends. To do so would be a one-way ticket to the Docklands. She had however acquiesced to Sofia's request and French lessons would take place for two hours every Wednesday morning.

Gradually life evolved into a leisurely-paced routine. Sofia formed real friendships with Elena and Helena and had good relationships with the other girls too, although Magda tended to keep herself to herself. Weekly visits from a hairdresser were a highlight, but the ultimate pleasure came from visiting the indoor swimming pool, which was located in an annex, next to the house.

During working hours, Sofia learned to detach herself from her body. She was now the highest priced option for customers and, while the other girls were told they had to attend the parties in Marseilles, Sofia was saved more and more for the wealthier clients who came to the house. After six months, she had accumulated over one hundred thousand francs in tips, which she kept in her underwear draw.

Occasionally the routine was interrupted when a customer got violent and had to be dragged off a girl and evicted. On one occasion an ambulance arrived at the front of the house with its lights flashing, and a plump man was carried out on a stretcher with an oxygen mask on his face. The old gent had suffered a heart attack while being flagellated in the bondage room.

There was one dark cloud on the horizon. The two Russians who had transported them from Cracow to France had started calling in at the brothel after they had delivered their cargo. They always insisted on having a threesome with Magda, who was forced to comply despite her protests.

Magda staggered groggily downstairs after these sessions, often with a black eye and other facial bruises. It was clear she had been given drugs.

Visits by the traffickers occurred every two months, and in between, Magda isolated herself from the other girls and sat staring into space for hours

One day Madame Lafarge told Sofia that she was next on the list for an apartment in Paris. With any luck, should be there before the end of winter. As a treat, she was taken on a shopping trip with Elena to Marseilles, and allowed to spend some of her tip money.

While they were sitting with their guard in a patisserie, Sofia's mind drifted back to the café in Cracow. She thought about Harris. But that life was gone forever. If she was lucky, perhaps she would find love again when she got to Paris.

The house was in chaos when they returned. Customers dressed hurriedly, preparing to leave, and all the girls were huddled together in the reception area, many of them in tears.

One of the new girls, Natalya spoke. 'The two Russians arrived unexpectedly. They paid some money and dragged Magda upstairs. She tried to escape but they were too strong for her. For the next twenty minutes we listened to her screams. Then it grew silent. Madame Lafarge told the security guards not to intervene as the Russians worked directly for Mr. Borizov. There was a loud bang and one of the Russians burst through the door, bleeding from a bullet wound in his stomach. The door slammed shut after him. Madame Lafarge yelled at us to go to our rooms, but we were too scared to move. It was horrible. I don't know if Magda is alive or dead.'

Escape

The full story came out at breakfast the next day. The Russians had tied Magda to the bed and whipped her, then stubbed out their cigarettes on her buttocks. They untied her, gave her a shot of heroin and raped her orally and anally until she lost consciousness, or so they thought. For when they were done, Magda grabbed a steel comb she'd hidden under her mattress and stabbed the nearest man in the neck. Blood spurted everywhere. She grabbed his gun and shot her other attacker, hitting him in the stomach.

By this time the security men had been alerted. One of them raced up the stairs, gun in hand and discovered one of the Russians crawling on his stomach along the landing, with a trail of blood behind him.

The other guard escorted the guests and girls from the other occupied rooms. Madame Lafarge made sure that the guests were refunded their money and given a 'freebie' voucher. Then she went upstairs to the room where Magda had locked the door.

'Come out ma Cherie. We know what happened. No one will harm you. Open the door and we'll look after you.'

'Fuck off you bitch!' came the retort from inside the room. 'I'll kill anyone who sets foot inside this room.'

Madame Lafarge signalled the security guards. One of them kicked the door open and they rushed into the room Magda discharged her remaining three bullets without hitting anything other than the walls. She was soon overpowered and carried out kicking and swearing.

Madame Lafarge ordered the guards to take her to the bondage room.

No clients were admitted the next day. The girls gossiped incessantly. No one had seen Magda or the Russians. Late that night, the front door opened and Borizov and Smyslov strode in with faces like thunder. Madame Lafarge looked extremely nervous as she showed them into her office.

After an hour Igor entered the reception room and told the girls they had to go to the Bondage room. When they entered the room they gasped. Magda was chained, naked, her body raised so that only her toes connected with the floor. She sobbed loudly and asked the girls to help her.

The fire was lit and a branding iron glowing amidst the coals. Borizov and Smyslov entered the room. They had discarded their suits and wore jogging pants and sleeveless tee shirts.

Borizov stepped forward. 'I want all of you to watch what is going to happen here closely. This Polish bitch has cost me two valuable employees and slowed down our transportation process. What they were doing to her does not matter. You girls are worth nothing to me, other than the money you bring. You are my slaves.'

No one could look him in the eye.

Smyslov walked over to Magda and caressed her face and her hair. Her eyes grew wide with fear. 'So you think you are tough. Let's see how tough you are.'
He yanked back her head and inserted a brace into her mouth. Magda gagged and twisted her head from side to side.

Smyslov produced a pair of pliers from his trouser pocket and waved them in front of Magda's terrified face. One by one he began to extract her teeth. After the fourth tooth Magda passed out, almost choking on a mouthful of blood and saliva.

When Smyslov finished, Borizov stepped forward with a bucket of water and threw it over the hapless Magda. The girls looked on, both horrified and fascinated.

Borizov picked up the most severe of the whips in the bondage rack and walked toward Magda. She was only half conscious and did not react when he pressed the handle of the whip in the small of her back, where the livid welts from her beating stood out against her pale skin.

Borizov started slowly, bringing low screams from Magda.
He increased the ferocity of the beating and after twenty
lashes Magda passed out. When he had finished, the skin
on her back was like raw meat.

Everyone thought that Magda's hell had ended, but it was
not to be. Smyslov pulled the branding iron from the fire and
walked toward her. Borizov held her hair back and spoke.
'You like tattoos, don't you Magda? Well, we hare going to
give you a special one.'

The iron glowed. The brand was shaped like an S. Borizov
took it from Smyslov and pressed it to Magda's forehead.
As her skin sizzled, she emitted a terrifying scream. Three of
the watching girls vomited.

Magda's body slumped forward. Smyslov stepped forward and felt for a pulse on her neck. He nodded a silent 'No.' to Borizov.

'Typical!' ranted Borizov. 'I can't even recover my investment in the bitch. Madame Lafarge had better work you all harder from now on!'

He stormed out, followed by Smyslov and the stunned girls made their way upstairs, many of them sobbing violently.

These events acted as a catalyst for Sofia. She had not thought seriously of escape, but from now on she became totally focused on the concept. After a few days, she introduced the topic in conversation with Jana when they were out for a walk. It was stupid to talk indoors as they both thought that their bedroom was bugged.

'I've been thinking about it too.' said Jana, 'I'm worried that they'll send me to the Docks soon. I've been here for over five years and I have no family or boyfriend to buy me out. And I don't believe that the last two women to leave bought themselves out like Lafarge said. If it was true, they would have said goodbye to the rest of us.'

They two women agreed to keep an eye out for anything that might create a possible opportunity and agreed that it was too dangerous to enlist the help of one of their regular clients.

One morning, as they were returning from their walk, Sofia noticed that the door behind the security desk was slightly ajar. She made a point of stopping to talk with the guard and used her position to look into the room she could see beyond the open door.

She watched as Madame Lafarge unlocked a large cupboard and removed handful of passports. She set one passport aside and locked the others away.

Sofia's heart skipped a beat. Without identity papers there was little chance of making a successful escape. She couldn't wait to tell Jana what she'd witnessed. Over the next two weeks the would-be jail-breakers began to formulate a plan. With a view to getting hold of the key to the front door and ideally keys to one of the cars that belonged to Madame Lafarge, they would cultivate a friendship with two of the guards, who manned the front door on rotation, a friendship that hinted more was on offer, The youngest guard, Peter, soon caught on and regularly took Jana into the room behind the desk for sex in the early hours each Wednesday and Friday. He didn't think anything of her requests for a drink beforehand.

She acquired some ketamine at one of the parties she had to attend, and everything was set for the girls to make their move.

There were no calendars in the house, but the girls found out from clients that it was late August. They decided to make their escape attempt on the coming Friday night, as clients often paid for a sleepover at weekends so there would be a good few cars outside. Jana was an expert at hot-wiring engines a relic from her teenage years.

One the appointed night, Jana crept down the stairs as soon as the house was quiet. Peter waited for her with a broad smile on his face. He'd already opened the door to the room where the passports were stored. He guided Jana through the opening with one hand, fondling her firm buttocks with the other.

'I'm feeling so randy.' he said, 'I've brought a gag so you can cry out if you want to my darling.'

'How about a drink first to get me in the mood?' said Jana. Peter smiled and went to the drinks cupboard. He brought back a bottle of wine and two glasses, which he set on a low table next to a luxurious armchair.

Jana pushed him back into the chair. She unbuttoned his trousers and pulled them off roughly, followed by his boxer shorts. 'Let's hope that tastes as good as it looks.' she said, staring at his erection as he lay back in the chair.

She undressed quickly, the tiny phial of ketamine concealed in her hand. She got down on all fours and swallowed Peter's erection and began to undulate her mouth, flicking out her tongue from time to time.

Peter gasped and fell back in the chair with his eyes closed. This was exactly what she had hoped for. It only took a second to empty the vial into his glass. He moaned loudly and Jana halted. 'Time for some refreshment Peter, before you cum in my mouth and deprive my cunt of its pleasure.'

They gulped down their wine and Jana pushed Peter back and straddled him. She began to gyrate, slowly at first, but gradually she increased the pace. He moaned loudly, then went limp beneath her

Jana checked his face. He was definitely unconscious. She dressed quickly, went to the door and opened it. Sofia was there, crouched behind the desk. She joined Jana in the room and used a poker from beside the open door to lever open the cupboard containing the passports. Inside, there were fifteen passports and with various sets of keys.

It only took them a minute to locate their documents and they left the room quickly. A quick search of the key rack behind the security desk identified the key for the front door and two sets of car keys, which Sofia guessed, were for the two black, four-by-four Range Rovers that the guards used.

 'Take both sets of keys.' said Sofia. 'That way they might not be able to follow us.'

Adrenaline raced through Sofia's chest as they eased the front door open and ran toward the first of the vehicles. Jana slipped into the driver's seat and turned the key in the ignition. The engine turned over with a rumble. Sofia looked back toward the house but no lights came on.

Jana released the handbrake and edged the car away from the front of the house, gaining speed, as the building grew smaller in the rear view mirror. She smoothly exited the estate and turned onto the road.

'Let's head for Marseilles and then follow motorway signs for Paris. We'll need to ditch this as soon as possible as they'll have the police looking for it. Between us we have enough money to catch a train to Paris, or we could hitch a lift from a service station.'

Sofia reasoned that the latter option was the better as there would be no witnesses left behind to tell where they were headed.

'What if we can't get someone to stop for us?' Jana said, and they both burst out laughing.

After twenty minutes they came to a major signpost that offered two choices of reaching Paris. The A7 was the major route that would take them through Lyon, while the alternative route headed east to Millau and then north via Clermont Ferrand and Orleans on the A75.

They plumped for the latter as it wasn't a toll road and there was likely to be more traffic, increasing their chances of getting a lift.

After two hours, there was no evidence of a pursuit, so they stopped at a service station and parked in well back the area designated for lorries.

They entered the cafeteria. It was just after six in the morning so customers were few and far between and most appeared to be lorry drivers,

'Let me try to get our lift as you managed our escape.' Said Sofia.

Jana smiled. 'As long as you don't promise a threesome!'

'Those days are over.' retorted Sofia.

She struck gold at the third table she visited. The first two drivers were not heading for Paris, but the third was and he said he would be glad of the company, plus, having two beautiful women in his cab would be good for his image. They would have to get out before he reached his depot however as it was against company rules to pick up passengers.

It was a long drive and both girls caught up on some of the sleep they'd missed the previous day. Pierre told them he had been married for over thirty years and had three children who had all left home. The runaways were careful not to give any personal details which could lead to them being traced in the future.

They had just passed a signpost that announced it was ninety five kilometres to Paris, when a news bulletin interrupted the music coming from the radio.

'The body of a man in his late twenties was found with three gunshot wounds, on the outskirts of Marseilles last night. Police are looking for two women in connection with the murder. The women are described as of medium height with blond hair, attractive and with eastern European accents. They are also in their twenties.'

The girls looked at each other with alarm in their eyes. Fortunately there was no reaction from Pierre, and it wasn't long before they entered the outskirts of Paris. Pierre asked them where they wanted to be dropped off.

'Beside a Railway or Metro station if possible.' said Jana.

Pierre complied with Jana's request and the girls were preparing to get out of the cab when he said, 'I would split up if I were you, and do something to change your appearance. There's need to worry about me. If you're the girls mentioned on the news, I can't believe that you have anything to do with the killing of that young man.'

Both girls blushed then gave him a hurried farewell kiss on both cheeks. 'Be safe.' were Pierre's last words.

Gay Paris

The girls decided to find a café and discuss their immediate future over a cappuccino. They agreed that the first priority was to find a reasonably priced hotel, where they could stay for a few nights and talk things over properly.

They walked around the streets adjacent to the Porte De Versailles station and decided upon D'hôtel Murat, which was in an unfashionable part of the fourteenth Arrondisement. They shared the cost of the three-night stay, which included a continental breakfast.

Exhausted, they collapsed on their beds. 'Frontier will never give up looking for us.' said Sofia. 'We should change our appearance as much we can and probably split up.'

'Agreed.' said Jana. 'And after that, do you have any plans?'

'I hope I can remain anonymous in Paris. Perhaps I'll get a job in a restaurant or a bar and settle down for a year or so.'

'That sounds good. Tomorrow, we could look for flats within easy reach of each other and then go job hunting.'

When they met in the hotel bar the following evening, laden with shopping bag, the girls hardly recognised each other. Jana long hair was now a red close-cut crop, and she wore a smart pair of spectacles. For her part, Sofia had become a brunette and acquired a diamond stud in her nose.

The next day was spent hunting for apartments. The area they were in was mid-range and paying a month's rent on a small, furnished apartment left them both with a significant hole in their finances.

They need not have worried however, as both got a job within three interviews, Sofia at an elegant haute cuisine restaurant, and Jana at a busy bar near the railway station, where the head barman spent most of the interview undressing her with his eyes.

After their first winter in Paris they saw less and less of each other. Jana moved in with the Head Barman and often turned up for their Saturday morning coffee with heavy make-up on her cheeks that looked more like camouflage than anything else to Sofia.

Sofia made the most of her days off and visited most of the museums in Paris and the palace at Versailles. She was frequently asked to dinner by customers in the restaurant, as well as nights out with the other staff. But the last two years had put her off romance and the waiters referred to her as the 'Ice Maiden'.

She was often overcome by homesickness and made up her mind to ring her sister, even though doing so might be dangerous. She bought two mobile phones. One was dedicated to family calls only. If there was the slightest hint that she was at risk, she would discard it.

She eventually plucked up courage to make the call on December twenty-sixth. After several rings her call was connected and her chest tightened as she recognized her sister's voice. 'This is Agnieska speaking.'

'It's me. Sofia.'

There was a silence for ten seconds, followed by the sound of sobbing. 'Where have you been? We thought you were dead.'

'How's mama?'

'Mama's dead. She was heartbroken by your disappearance and wilted away. She died on the fifteenth of July last year.'

Sofia began to sob. 'I could not help it Agnieska. I could not help it. I was kidnapped.'

'Your boyfriend came round a week after you vanished. He reported your disappearance to the police but they weren't interested. Where are you living now?'

Sofia hesitated. 'I can't say Agnieska. I don't want to put you in danger. Is it all right if I ring you every Sunday evening? It is so good hearing your voice.'

'OK. I will make a point of staying in. Take care my darling sister.'

The calls went on for several weeks and Sofia let slip that she was living in Paris. Agnieska asked if they could meet and promised not to tell anyone.

Sofia let her loneliness take charge and the sisters made plans to meet at Starbucks outside the main entrance to Gare de L'Est station at five pm in two weeks' time.

The next week flew by and Sofia arrived at Starbucks half an hour early, having reconnoitered the area first. She had not seen anything or anyone that set alarm bells ringing. She spotted Agnieska leaving the station and ran to greet her sister.

They hugged and wiped the tears away from each other's cheeks. 'You look so different. So much thinner.' Agnieska said.

'That's what life on the run does to you.' Sofia replied.

Over a cappuccino they talked constantly. Then Sofia said,' Let's go to my flat. I've cooked a meal for you. My cooking has improved enormously since I began working at the restaurant.'

In thirty minutes they were at her apartment. She showed Agnieska into the bedroom and told her she would sleep on the sofa bed in the living room. Agnieska protested but Sofia would have none of it.

As Agnieska was unpacking Sofia called out, 'I'll just pop to the corner shop for a bottle of wine. Do you still prefer white?'

Agnieska affirmed and Sofia ran off to make her purchase. She had her usual exchange of conversation with Monsieur

Gerard behind the counter and set off on the return journey. She got no further than fifty yards when her heart stopped.

A black four-by-four Range Rover screeched to a halt in front of the apartment and three muscular men climbed out. Sofia gasped. She recognized two of them as they headed for the entrance. Borizov and Smyslov!

She tried frantically to ring Agnieska to warn her but there was no answer, so she concealed herself in an alley that gave her a view of the apartments and waited. For a little while all was quiet. Then there was a loud scream and a woman's body hurtled through the air and smashed onto the pavement.

Less than thirty seconds later, the three men came running out of the building, got into the car and drove off. Sofia ran across the road as fast as she could, toward Agnieska's body, which lay face down on the concrete.

There was blood everywhere. She slowly turned her sister's body over. Agnieska's nose was smashed and her neck and legs were at a strange angle, but amazingly she still appeared to be breathing. Sofia sobbed violently but leaned over as she saw that Agnieska was trying to speak. 'There was a tracker on my suitcase. I did not tell them anything.' Then a fountain of blood erupted from Agnieska's mouth and she lay silent.

'Don't leave me,' sobbed Sofia but it was no good. There was no pulse in her sister's neck.

Sofia was in an absolute panic but her rational brain took over. She couldn't take the risk of going back to her flat or the restaurant. She needed to leave Paris as soon as possible and without leaving a trail. Thank goodness she had her handbag with her and inside it her bank card and passport.

Three hours later she was on the Eurostar heading to London. En route she rang Jana and told her what had happened, promising to call again in a week's time. Then she fell asleep. She woke with a start as the ticket collector touched her shoulder and said 'London in five minutes Madame.'

Salvation

Sofia felt refreshed by her nap. She alighted from the train at St Pancras and went to find a café as she had missed her evening meal.

An hour with a cappuccino and omelette and chips stimulated her thought processes.

The first thing that struck her was that apart from Jana, she was alone in the world. But Sofia did not believe in feeling sorry for herself, and at least she had her passport and over five thousand euros.

She walked to the nearest bookshop, bought an atlas and a Fodor's guide to the British Isles, and returned to the coffee shop to think.

She had some important decisions to make. The first was where should she live? She knew little about the UK but she decided that she was better off living outside London. Paris had been a lonely place for her and had not given her the anonymity she craved. Worst of all, it had claimed the life of her sister.

It would pay to live somewhere that would enable her to travel back to Europe or Poland easily if she wished. Perhaps the South Coast could offer her that opportunity. She thought of getting a train to Brighton but after reading her guidebook she plumped for Chichester. There were a number of good restaurants there and she should be able to find work.

Within a week, Sofia had a job as a waitress at a fine dining restaurant on the edge of Chichester and a rented room above a pub. Having ditched her mobile phones in France she now had a new iPhone, although she had very few names in her address book.

Time passed, and she changed her accommodation at the end of the three-month rental period. She answered an advertisement in a newspaper for someone wishing to share a two bedroomed apartment.

Her landlady, Sylvia, was a solicitor. The arrangement worked out well as Sylvia spent most weekends at her boyfriend's house. She totally respected Sofia's privacy though secretly she wondered why such a beautiful woman was so alone.

Winter came and went and cherry blossom was beginning to cascade slowly onto the wide avenues in the town centre. En route to work Sofia passed the frontage of a shop, Coral

Bookmakers, which was advertising for part-time daytime and evening staff.

Sofia currently worked five evenings each week, including every Saturday night, but her shifts did not begin until six in the evening. She went inside and asked to see the manager, a woman, who asked Sofia if she had any experience of working in a betting shop or handling and accounting for cash.

A week later she received a letter from Coral and was surprised to see she had been offered the post of Part Time Summer Cashier.

Sofia reported for duty the following Tuesday and began her training under the watchful eye of the manager, Margaret. It wasn't easy work, as there tended to be a rush of customers to the tills just before a race began, which put the cashiers under extreme pressure. But Sofia gradually became proficient and enjoyed the daily banter with the customers, most of whom were 'safe' old men.

She learned about Goodwood festival when Chichester bulged at the seams with race-goers, hotels and restaurants were fully booked and her tips were ten times the normal weekly amount at the restaurant. It was the same story at Coral. There were more customers than ever, all eager to place their bets.

One evening she was working at the restaurant when a group of inebriated men turned up, flush from their day's winnings. They were seated at one of Sofia's tables where they made vulgar remarks at increasing volume. Diners on neighbouring tables glowered and left early as the noise and vulgarity levels escalated. The headwaiter asked the group to tone things down but he was in his sixties and was clearly intimidated.

Sofia began to dread her visits to the table, as a number of lewd remarks were directed at her, and hands had begun to wander. She was glad when she was asked to bring the bill, along with coffee and mints.

She arrived at the table and asked which of the men wanted the bill. One of them lurched to his feet. 'Give it to me darling and there's an extra five hundred quid tip if you come back to my hotel and give me some of what you're hiding under that uniform.'

Sofia blushed and turned away. The man grabbed her by the arm 'Don't you ignore me, you stuck up bitch!' He drew back his free hand to slap her across the face.

But before he could deliver the blow his arm was grabbed and twisted behind his back. A gentleman who'd been sitting alone at one of her tables moved swiftly to grab the loudmouth.

'Now then,' said the stranger, 'I think it's time you apologised to the lady and you and your cronies paid up and left. And make sure you leave a bloody good tip!'

They men could not leave fast enough. One of them opened his mouth to issue a threat, but one look in the stranger's eyes and the words dried up in his throat.

Sofia approached her rescuer who had re-seated himself.
 'Thank you for rescuing me.'

She looked at him closely and saw that he was tall and slim, sandy haired and dressed in comfortable but expensive clothes. 'It was my pleasure.' he said.

He turned his face towards her and gave a slow smile. He had piercing blue eyes that seemed to look right into her. 'I'm Stewart.' he said, extending his hand.

It was a long time since Sofia had experienced sexual feelings, but that night, as she lay in bed, the stranger's face kept coming into view and she experienced that long forgotten warmth in the pit of her stomach.

She reported for work as usual at six, ready to manage her half dozen tables and her heart skipped a beat when she saw Stewart enter and make his way to the same seat. The night seemed to race by as he worked his way through three courses and a good bottle of wine, followed by coffee and amaretto.

They chatted on and off during the meal and Sofia could feel the attraction growing whenever he looked at her. At eleven pm his was the only table occupied. 'Is there anything else I can get you sir?' she asked, feeling the blood rush to her cheeks.

'As a matter of fact there is.' He smiled and looked directly at her as he pulled two tickets from his inside jacket pocket. 'I have a horse running at the Goodwood festival tomorrow and I wondered if you would be my guest for the day?'

Sofia was taken aback. 'I'll be at work, I would love to come but I won't be able to get the time off.'

'If you mean your job at Coral and here at the restaurant, I have spoken to the managers and told them that you have this opportunity. They both said for you not to worry about taking the time off. Please forgive me for being presumptuous, but I used to work in army intelligence and I don't believe in leaving anything to chance, especially not when something is important to me.

If Sofia had blushed previously she went bright red now. However, before she could say no, Stewart reached into his inside pocket and pulled out a photograph of a horse

'This is Chevalier, my pride and joy. Please come and help me support him tomorrow in his most important race to date. No strings attached.'

It looked like game, set and match. Sofia nodded and said 'How will I get there?'

'Give me your address and I'll pick you up. Wear your best outfit. It's quite a social occasion.'

As she walked home Sofia's mind was in a whirl. To her surprise, Sylvia was sitting in the living room watching TV. 'I have to work overtime tomorrow so it wasn't worth going to James' flat. You're back late. Let me pour you a glass of wine.'

As she sipped her wine, Sofia blurted out what had happened that evening. She told Sylvia that she didn't have suitable clothes.

'That's easily fixed,' said Sylvia. 'This calls for a shopping expedition and a quick visit to the hairdressers first thing tomorrow morning. Don't worry. You'll be back here and ready on time. This is so exciting, not to mention romantic. You simply must invite me to the wedding!'

Not for the first time that evening, Sofia felt her cheeks flushing.

The following morning was a whirlwind. Sylvia woke her at seven with coffee and toast and took her to a hairdresser that opened at eight, where she had a wash and blow-dry. This was followed by another coffee as they waited for the boutiques to open.

One hour later, Sofia was back in the apartment, having a hot shower before getting dressed. She looked at her naked body in the mirror and asked herself, 'Am I damaged goods?'

She had never given into the oppression of her circumstances, but now, faced with the possibility of having a real relationship, she told herself she would not give Stewart any false hope of becoming her lover. Firm in her resolve, she zipped up the gorgeous silk dress Sylvia had bought for her and waited for Stewart to pick her up.

They enjoyed a marvellous day. Stewart showed her around the stands and paddock at Goodwood, and she marvelled at the beauty of the racecourse. After the tour there was a champagne lunch, and then the main event of the day. Chevalier's race was at five minutes past three. A one mile, three-year old handicap for which he was five-to-one, second favourite. He looked magnificent in the pre-parade area, with his coat and eyes gleaming.

Stewart suggested she had a ten pound each way bet and took her to the row of bookmakers in front of the stands, where she surprised him by walking up and down the line looking for the best price, something she was familiar with from her job at Corals. He left her briefly, telling her he was going to place bets of his own.

Sofia had never had a personal involvement in a horse-race, but she found herself jumping up and down and urging Chevalier on as he came from the back of the field to forge into the lead a furlong from the finish, and pull away to win by two lengths. She was red faced with the excitement of it all as she collected her eighty pounds.

'You can bet with me any time darling!' said the bookmaker as she collected her winnings. She turned away to see a bookmaker further down the line counting out many hundreds of pounds and handing it to Stewart. Then she experienced déjà vu, as he walked up to two other bookmakers and collected more fistfuls of cash.

Stewart asked her to pose with him for photographs in the winning enclosure, but last thing she wanted was to appear in the press. Stewart seemed disappointed but shrugged it off.

They spent the rest of the afternoon getting to know each other. Sofia said she'd worked in the restaurant trade in Cracow, Paris and then Chichester, but left out her kidnapping and time in the brothel

In turn, Stewart told her his story. He'd had been a major in the Army until five years ago and had seen a lot of the world, until he resigned for personal reasons. He found he had a lot of time on his hands and started share trading and sports betting while he waited to start a civilian career. He found that he had a real aptitude for it and postponed his return to proper 'work' several times. Five years on, he employed two stock traders and threw himself full time into his sports betting which took him all over the world.

They enjoyed each other's company so much that Sofia did not hesitate when Stewart suggested they go to his hotel for an evening meal. A tingle ran through her as he placed his hand on her upper back and guided her through the exit doors.

Neither of them ate much. They were too busy gazing into each other's eyes. When Stewart placed his hand on hers asked her if she would like to come up to his room for a nightcap, Sofia realized she was lost.

As soon as they entered Stewart's suite, they fell into each other's arms and were soon naked in bed. Stewart was a gentle and considerate lover and she used her experience to ensure that he entered her in different positions on three occasions. After his final explosion inside her, they held each other close until he drifted off to sleep and she turned away so that he couldn't see her tears. They were tears of joy, something she was unaccustomed to, like his long slow kisses. She had not kissed anyone since her night with Harris.

So much for her resolve, she thought, as she finally fell asleep.

They saw each other most weekends over the remainder of the summer, with regular outings to the races, which Sofia enjoyed almost as much as Stewart. He took her to see the three horses he owned at Brian Meehan's stables in Lambourn. She loved everything about these visits, though most of all she enjoyed learning how the horses were cared for and the details of the training process,

Winter approached and Stewart planned to be away for most of November, visiting the USA for the Breeders' Cup, followed by Australia for the Melbourne Cup and two weeks in Hong Kong for their international season.

Their meetings were almost always in hotels, with occasional weekends in Sofia's apartment. Sofia didn't mind as she felt she did not have to give total commitment to their relationship. Not that she ever thought of seeing someone else.

Then one weekend in late September, it happened. Stewart turned to her in bed and looked into her eyes. 'I love you Sofia and I want you to move in with me.'

She was shocked. 'I can't. What about my jobs?'

'Give them up. I'll pay you to keep my trading and betting records, and, if you are not offended, to look after my house.'

Sofia didn't know what to say. She could see that Stewart was disappointed she had not given him a quick answer. After a few moments she told him it was such a big decision that she would like a week to think it over, but that she would give him her answer the following Friday. Ever the gentleman, Stewart agreed.

The following week was torture. Sofia's thoughts ranged t and fro. One minute she planned to run away, the next to listen to her conscience. Eventually, she decided to tell Stewart the truth about her life over the last few years. He deserved to know what he was getting and she was prepared for the worst.

Friday evening arrived and he was waiting for her in the hotel lobby with a large gin and tonic on the table in front of him

'This is my condemned man expression. Please give me your decision quickly and put me out of my misery.'

While she was making herself comfortable, Stewart ordered her a drink. Sofia began hesitantly but gradually told him the story of her years as a sex slave. She did not know how he would react but noticed tears rolling slowly down his cheeks. When she'd finished, he put his hand on hers and said 'My poor darling. Let me spend the rest of my life helping to make up to you for the hand you've been dealt in life.'

'I'm spoiled goods. I don't deserve your love.'

'Would it make it easier if I told you I had a secret too?'

She nodded and he told her about the time six years ago when he was serving in Afghanistan, and his wife and eight year old daughter were killed in a road accident. Sophia gasped and reached out to him.

'Until the night I met you in the restaurant, my life was a desert.'

Now both of them were in tears. Abandoning the idea of dinner, they spent the rest of the night entwined in each other's arms, sharing their innermost feelings.

Sofia moved in the following weekend. When she handed in her notice her colleagues wished her well and asked her to send them invitations to the wedding.

She accompanied Stewart on his tour, which turned out to be more like a honeymoon. He was shell-shocked but deliriously happy when she told him that she was pregnant, three weeks after they returned. 'It's the best Christmas present I've had.'

Sofia wanted to learn how to ride but agreed to wait until after their child was born, and over the next few months Stewart gradually extracted details of her kidnapping and imprisonment.

An antenatal scan revealed she was carrying a boy, but highlighted one or two problems, so she was told that she would need regular check ups in the final three months, and admittance to hospital in the month before the baby was due.

Shortly before she was due to leave for hospital, Sofia received a call from Jana. They had spoken on several occasions since Sofia arrived in England.

Jana was now in Rome. She too had met someone and said that he was 'The one.'

Sofia could tell that Jana was excited and after the usual preliminaries her friend wasted no time. 'My brother rang me from Poland. The bodies of the two Russians who managed Frontier were found in the basement of their office building. Both had been stripped and beaten and there was an S burned into their foreheads. It was all over the TV news. Do you understand? It means we can go back to Poland!'

That night at dinner, Sofia told Stewart the news. She looked at him closely for a reaction. There was a moment's silence and then he spoke. 'Couldn't happen to two nicer

people!'

PART TWO

POLLYS STORY

Life As An Equestrian

'Come on Spartan!' Polly whispered in her horse's ear. 'Only three fences to go.'

Her bay gelding had started the cross-country course in thirtieth position that morning, but as an ex-steeplechaser, he loved this discipline and she knew he was the fastest horse in the field. She could see the finishing chute in the distance and there was no sign of Gay Spartan slowing. The next fence came sharp left and downhill.

Spartan's momentum made him over jump. Polly's heart was in her mouth as she was pitched forward on his neck. She could hear the gasp from the spectators, but it was followed by applause that faded behind her, as her pride and joy found another leg from somewhere and picked himself up without depositing her on the turf.

There were only four hundred yards left now. She let Spartan have his head and he winged the last two fences. Polly heard the announcer as she crossed the finishing line.

'A clear round in the fastest time of the day for Gay Spartan and his young rider Polly Townsend!'

As soon as she reached the unsaddling enclosure she dismounted quickly and fetched a bucket of water for Spartan to drink, then two more, which she used to douse his heaving flanks.

It wasn't long before her excited parents arrived. 'Well done Polly! You're in first place for the cross country and second place overall.' exclaimed her father.

Her mother hugged her with a tear in her eye.

'Who's a clever boy then?' she said, hugging the horse around the neck. Spartan seemed to know what he had done and shook his head and whinnied.

Next to arrive were her two friends, Rachel and Caroline, 'Brilliant, just brilliant!' said the girls in harmony, going on to make a fuss of Spartan.

The friends had been inseparable since they met at school. Polly was engaged to Rachel's brother, Greg, who was currently serving a second tour in Afghanistan.

After settling Spartan Polly joined her parents and the girls in the tea tent. An earnest looking young man approached the table

'Polly Llewellyn?' he enquired. 'My name is Peter Sands. I'm from the Midhurst and Petworth Observer. Can you spare me five minutes?'

Polly blushed. She was essentially a shy person, but a broad smile broke out on her face when the reporter told her she was in second place going into tomorrow's final round of show jumping. The young reporter was shocked when she told him that this was her first competitive three-day event.

Peter told her that the first five finishers would get automatic entry to the national championships at Hickstead in three months time and the first four finishers in that competition would be chosen to ride for Great Britain in the Olympics.

Polly's father James spoke saying ' No celebrating for you tonight my girl, its early to bed, you have a big day tomorrow.'

The following morning Polly was up bright and early and was soon on her way to the stables where she rented a box for Spartan. The co-owner of the stables, Jessica, greeted her with a cheery, 'Good morning!' which Polly returned.

'You gave Spartan a great ride yesterday. You've got real talent. Have you ever thought about becoming an amateur jockey?'

Jessica and her husband, Richard, had worked with Spartan for the past two years and were extremely proud of his progress.

'Any last minute advice?' asked Polly.

'Keep calm. Focus. You've got a great horse. Together you can do it. It's about control. Make sure he doesn't go too fast and you'll be fine.'

Polly and her dad put Spartan into a horsebox and made the two-hour trip to Ardingley, where they busied themselves settling the powerful horse. They watched as Roberta Clifford-Pemberton passed by with her entourage. An Olympic champion, Roberta had a stable of twenty horses, funded by her millionaire father. She swaggered arrogantly straight into Polly's path.

'Well done yesterday lass!' said Roberta's father. 'Shame our Roberta hasn't got the bottle for cross country.'

Roberta scowled and blurted, 'Lets see how she does in the showjumping with that racehorse. Twenty faults is my guess.'

Polly shrugged as the show-jumping star stomped away.

Then it was time to groom Spartan and ready herself for the competition. She glanced at the scoreboard, noting that she was only four points adrift of Roberta, who was currently in the lead on sixteen faults.

Polly and her father had walked the course three times. It was definitely the toughest she'd encountered so far. Spartan was an excellent jumper but didn't respond well to excessive restraint. The two doubles, where fences were set close together, were a definite challenge.

After watching other riders make their round, it was Polly's turn. She trotted Spartan towards the start and the butterflies in her stomach evaporated in favour of a steely determination. She bent over the head of her mount and whispered, 'Come on Spartan. Show them all what you can do.'

The buzzer sounded and the most important two minutes of Polly's life began. There were sixteen fences, with almost as many twists and turns. A gasp came from the packed crowd when Spartan soared over the first fence at twice the speed of those that had gone before.

Polly had an important decision to make. Either she reined him in hard and took each fence in a measured fashion, or she let him have his head. She didn't think too long. She chose the latter.

Thirty seconds later the whole arena erupted. Spartan had gone clear in by far the fastest time of the day. Polly's heart was in her mouth when he rapped the top bar of the second fence of the second double, but it remained in place after wobbling precariously for what seemed like an age.

She dismounted swiftly and gave Spartan a big hug and a large drink of water. 'Who's a clever boy then? It's extra carrots for you this week!'

Spartan nodded his head several times in quick succession as if he'd understood.

Polly rushed back to the auditorium in time to watch the second half of Roberta's round. She admired the smooth precision of horse and rider and the effortless way in which they negotiated the steep turns. Only four fences remained, including the second double, and the pair had not made a single mistake.

They cleared the first part of the double, and then it happened. The horse seemed unsure as to how many strides it should take before jumping the second part and got too close to the fence, dislodging the top barrier.

It was all over. Polly had won the cup.

She went over immediately to congratulate Roberta, who jumped off her horse, face twisted with rage. She was about to strike her horse with her whip when a tall stranger emerged from the crowd and grabbed her hand in mid air. 'That's no way to treat a horse. You should know that!'

He stared intensely at Roberta. She went scarlet and stormed off, leaving the horse without any water, and it was Polly who had to fetch the tired animal a drink.

The stranger was still holding the horse when she returned with a brimming bucket. 'Well done. You have a magnificent thoroughbred there, ' he said in a slightly Latin accent.

She looked up into a tanned face, with the most amazing blue eyes, and felt herself colouring up. She managed to blurt out, 'Thank you,' and went even redder when she felt those eyes appraising her from top to tail.

He gave her a dazzling smile and held out his hand. 'Hector Sanchez, pleased to make your acquaintance.'

She felt a shiver go through her body but managed to introduce herself without making any mistakes.

'You need to go and collect your prize.' he said and turned away slowly with a smile on his face, as though he knew the effect he had on her.

The prize giving was a blur. Roberta had a sour face throughout and never spoke one world of congratulation to Polly.

Afterwards, Polly only had time for a quick shower before it was time to get ready for that evening's Hunt Ball. She was about to call Greg to let him know the exciting news, but decided to wait until the following day.

The evening was a whirl of congratulations, photographs and one or two more drinks than she would normally consume, courtesy of Caroline and Rachel.

Then it was time for the Champions' Waltz. Long-held tradition was for the winner of the trials to dance a waltz with his or her partner and in Greg's absence Polly had arranged to take the floor with her father.

She was just about to walk off the floor when she felt a touch on her arm. She turned and looked into the smiling face of Hector Sanchez. 'Perhaps you would do me the honour of the next dance.' he said.

Polly found herself being gently propelled onto the dance floor. Hector smiled again. 'Such a waste, for a beautiful woman like you to have to dance with her father.'

He was a superb dancer and she felt herself floating across the floor and relaxing more and more into his strong arms. The music came to an end and Hector spoke. 'I'd better not monopolise you or tongues will wag. But perhaps you'll do me the honour of introducing me to your parents?'

Completely in his thrall, Polly complied. Hector introduced himself formally to her father and stooped to kiss the women on their hands. Rachel and Caroline looked at her, mouthing improper suggestions as Hector continued. 'I'm a big admirer of your daughter's horsemanship. I'm over in England to play in the International Polo Tournament next weekend and would be delighted if you would be my guests.'

Polly's father said that they would be pleased to take up the invitation and Polly could not suppress a feeling of jealousy as Hector danced twice with Caroline and Rachel during the rest of the evening.

She woke later than usual the next morning and felt guilty about the warm feeling in the pit of her stomach when she thought about Hector. She turned her thoughts to Greg instead, and their easy friendship which had grown into romance.

Greg was her only boyfriend, and their first weekend together in a hotel was not a wholehearted success. She failed to achieve an orgasm when they had sex, but reasoned that this was something that would come with the passage of time. Greg left for Afghanistan the following week and proposed via satellite after he had been there for a month.

Polly noticed how tired Gregg looked whenever he called her and so she said yes. Afterward, lying in bed, she wondered whether she'd done so more out of sympathy than love. And now it was time to Skype him and tell him her news.

She noticed the bandage wrapped around his wrist but Gregg laughed it off. He was thrilled by her news and joked that he would have to get used to taking third place in her life after Spartan.

He asked her to book somewhere romantic for the weekend after he arrived home the following month, and she told him that she couldn't wait, and they ended the call.

Betrayal

The following week Polly slipped into her usual routine of early mornings at the stables, followed by regular hours at Lloyds bank in Midhurst where she worked as a Customer Services Assistant.

Many of her regular customers passed on their congratulations and she had even better news when the Branch Manager Mr. Wilson called her into his office on Wednesday morning.

The board members were delighted with her performance at the weekend and the bank would sponsor travel and expenses for the next two years. In addition, she wouldn't need to book annual leave to attend future competitions.

The week was drawing to close when Polly had a surprise visitor. She looked up from her desk in the bank's foyer and Roberta's father, Bob Clifford-Pemberton, looked down at her with a broad smile on his face.

'Hello lass. How are you? Has the excitement of the weekend worn off yet?'

He invited her to join him for tea after she finished work. Bob was alone at a quiet corner table when she entered the Copper Kettle, shortly after five o'clock. She took a seat opposite him as he stood up to welcome her. He asked her how Spartan was and some questions about the horse's feeding and training regimes which Polly enjoyed discussing with him.

'Right then, lass. I'll get down to the main reason I came today. I've spent a fortune setting up the leading equestrian business in the United Kingdom. Roberta has played her part, winning several major domestic and international show jumping competitions.' He looked directly at her as he spoke these words and continued 'However, we've failed to enjoy the same success in eventing, despite several expensive acquisitions. After watching you and Spartan on Saturday, I know what's been missing.'

Polly but had an awful feeling about what was coming next.

'In all the time I've been in this game, I've never seen such a natural as Spartan. No disrespect to you lass, but he could win any cross-country competition anywhere in the world, no matter who was riding him. Name your price and it's yours.'

Polly glared at him. 'Spartan is not for sale at any price.'

'Everything in life has its price. How about if I offer you thirty thousand pounds, plus the pick of any of my existing horses as a replacement.'

'I can only repeat what I said. He is not for sale at any price.' Polly extended her hand and rose to leave.

'How about fifty thousand pounds?'

Polly walked toward the exit without turning back when Bob's final words reached her. 'That's not a wise move. Horses' careers can end in an instant. They're not safe even running around their paddocks at home.'

Polly looked straight at him. A sneer spread across his lips. 'Don't come near me or Spartan again.'

She went home and told her father what had happened.

'Mr. Clifford-Pemberton is clearly used to getting his own way. We need to treat Spartan's security as a priority.'

Two hours later, Polly and her father sat in Jessica's living room. Her husband, Richard, joined them.

'I'll call him and tell him what I think of him, and what I'll do to him if anything untoward happens to Spartan.' Richard said

'It's his word against Polly's,' her father replied. 'We need to see if we can strengthen physical security here at the stables.'

'We'll install additional lighting and CCTV and relocate Spartan in the box nearest to our house,' said Richard.

Everyone was satisfied with these measures and Polly and her father drove home, where she spent a restless night thinking about the day's events, and her forthcoming date with Hector. Try as she might she could not rid herself of thoughts about what it would be like for him to hold her again.

The following morning she took an age to dress and groom herself and applied a touch more of her favourite perfume than was usual.

Polly and her family arrived at Windsor Polo Park shortly after one o'clock and were escorted to the VIP lunch tent. They'd barely taken their seats and ordered an aperitif when Hector came striding towards their table. In shiny brown boots, camel jodhpurs and a cream polo shirt, he looked even more handsome than Polly remembered. She swallowed hard and tried valiantly to slow her heart rate.

Hector flashed that perfect smile and kissed her hand, and she her face beginning to redden.

'The match begins at three o'clock,' said Hector. 'I'm in the Rest of The World Team. We play against Prince Charles' Select. It should be an excellent match. Several of the world's top polo players are taking part. I'll after your lunch and escort you to your seats.'

Hector bowed his farewell and made his way to the exit, Polly couldn't help but notice that most of the women's eyes followed him.

True to his word, Hector returned shortly before two pm. They followed him to the VIP area. They were about to take their seats when Hector said, 'Please excuse me Mr. and Mrs. Townsend, but several of my colleagues would like to meet your daughter. She's quite famous now in equestrian circles.'

Hector took Polly's hand firmly in his and led her off in the direction of a cluster of tents, on the far side of the field. He guided her through the flap of the first one. It was empty except for a series of chaise lounges and sofas.

'What are we doing here? You said you were taking me to meet your teammates.' said Polly.

'There's plenty of time for that, but it's time we got to know each other.' He spun her round and pulled her forward. She tried to protest but his lips were on her neck and she felt his hot breath on her.

She tried to push him away but he was far too strong and continued to hold her. Then he pushed her back onto the nearest couch. 'Stop. Please.' she pleaded, but his hands began to unbutton her dress and his mouth found her erect nipples as he murmured with satisfaction.

She gasped as he continued to explore her, slipping off her panties and inserting his fingers into her. 'No. No. Not here.' she moaned, but he was oblivious to her pleading.

He began to use his tongue on her, licking her clitoris at alternating speeds. She could not help it and came in his face.

He smiled at her and forced her thighs apart, stepping back to remove his boots and jodhpurs. He thrust into her and she gasped again. In the next twenty minutes, she came twice more as he manipulated her like a marionette.

'You're mine now Polly. I have to travel to Spain after the match today, but give me your mobile number and we'll spend a weekend together in Spain soon.'

She reached for her panties and dress, anything to cover up her nakedness and vulnerability. Hector bade her goodbye, with a long, slow kiss.

Polly's mind was in a turmoil but she dressed and adjusted her make up as best as she could, then made for the Ladies' tent. 'Are you all right dear? You look a little flushed.' Polly's mum said as she rejoined her.

'I'm out of breath after running back from the player's tent.'

The match was breathlessly exciting for the crowd who, but not for Polly, whose conscience berated her, telling her that she'd betrayed Gregg and behaved like a whore. The match ended and Hector was voted best player. He left the field shortly without retuning to their group.

 It was several nights before Polly slept well and she was far less talkative than usual in her calls to Gregg. He failed to notice and told her that he had to stay in Afghanistan for another month, as there was a big push on.

Three weeks passed and there was no call from Hector. More worryingly her period was late. She became increasingly desperate, as she knew Hector had not used a condom, and she didn't use any form of regular birth control.

Her only release was when she rode out Spartan. By the time Hickstead arrived, she had purchased a pregnancy kit and knew the worst. The test confirmed she was seven weeks pregnant. She had two big decisions to make. Have an abortion or tell Gregg what had happened and beg his forgiveness.

She managed to pull herself together in time for the dressage competition and ended the day half way down the field, which was what she had anticipated. Roberta was in the lead and she basked in the media attention.

Polly chatted idly to Rachel and Caroline after the competition, covering up the growing panic inside her. She was about to join her father to go home when Caroline blurted out, 'God alert!'

Polly turned round and saw Hector striding toward them. He made a show of greeting all three girls before saying, 'Polly, are you going to take me to see that wonderful horse of yours?'

She told the girls she would see them tomorrow and led Hector to where Spartan was paddocked, closely guarded by Richard. Some fifty yards before Spartan, she stopped and turned to Hector with tears in her eyes. 'Why haven't you called me? Don't you care about me?' she blurted as tears rolled down her cheeks.

'I'm sorry my darling. I've had a major crisis at my company and it took all of my attention to resolve it. Of course I care about you.'

She wanted to be in his arms, but the fact they were in a public area held her back.

'I'm staying to watch until the competition ends. Come to dinner with me and stay the night at my hotel on Sunday night. Hopefully we'll have plenty to celebrate'

Polly decided she would use that occasion to tell him about the baby. She'd have to create an excuse for not being at home that night.

That evening, she slept properly for the first time in weeks, and was up bright and early seeing to Spartan. Today was going to be the most important day of their lives.

As usual her father got them to the venue early and they went for a cup of tea and to discuss the lay out of the course, leaving Caroline to keep an eye on Spartan.

Polly had the course firmly imprinted on her mind and felt that it would suit Spartan well, as it was longer than most and the fences were slightly more spread out. There were three tricky entries where there was a sharp downhill descent on approach.

After their discussion, Polly and her father found Spartan alone. There was no sign of Caroline, who turned up a few moments later.

'Where were you?' asked Polly.

'I'm sorry I left him, but I was bursting for a pee.'

Thirty minutes Polly was on her way to the starting line. Her heart buoyed at the sight of Hector smiling encouragement at her from his place in the crowd.

The start buzzer sounded and they were on their way. They had travelled less than a mile when Polly sensed that all was not well with Spartan. Normally he was throwing his head around in between fences, anxious to accelerate. Today he felt labored and was far less extravagant than usual at his fences.

It seemed a real effort for him to clear the more difficult fences and Polly realized they were incurring time penalties. She noticed Spartan's breath was getting more labored and whispered words of encouragement to him.

They approached the first downhill section of the course, which had a tricky chicane following a tough fence located on the decline. She knew something was wrong when Spartan didn't steady himself and travelled far too quickly into the downhill fence.

She tried valiantly to pull him up, but it was too late. He crashed into the fence and sent her catapulting through the air. Spartan followed her down the slope, rolling over with his full body weight pressing on his back legs.

There was a collective gasp from the crowd and the marshals began to wave red flag, directing the next horse around the fence.

Polly tried to get up, but screamed when she put her weight on her left leg that protruded beneath her at a strange angle.

Worse followed as Spartan tried and failed to raise himself off the ground. Screens were erected around him and within two minutes a vet had arrived.

Two paramedics began to check her out. 'Your leg is definitely broken and we think that you have two broken ribs and bruising to the base of your spine.'

Polly wouldn't let them take her away from the scene. She sobbed violently as she waited to see whether Spartan had survived.

Her father and mother came running toward her with concern etched deeply into their faces. 'Are you alright darling?' her mother said, taking hold of her hand and holding it against her heaving chest.

'Daddy. Please go and see how Spartan is doing.' she implored.

Her father ran off toward the screens. It was five minutes before he emerged. He came slowly toward them with his head bowed and tears rolling down his cheeks. 'There was nothing they could do. He'd shattered a fetlock.'

'Take me to him. I want to say goodbye.' said Polly, and the paramedics carried her over.

Spartan had been tranquilised for the pain, but the termination had not yet taken place. Despite the agonising pain in her leg, Polly pulled herself up and took his head in her hands, showering his face with kisses. 'My darling Spartan, you will stay in my mind forever.'

She stayed until the vet put his hand on her shoulder and told her it was time. She didn't stay for the end. She wanted to remember her horse as he was, striding out across the moors, tossing his head and full of the joys of nature. Taking her leave, she asked the vet's assistant if they would undertake a blood test and notify her of the findings.

She emerged from the screens to see Hector running towards her. He raced up to her and took her in his arms, oblivious of who might be watching.

'My poor darling.' he whispered, holding her tight and smothering her with kisses. Polly could see her mother, father and Caroline over Hector's shoulder. They were looking at each other in total shock.

'I'll come and see you in hospital tonight.' said Hector.

'It's time to go love.' said the lead paramedic.

Her mother came up to the stretcher. 'I'll go in the ambulance with you.'

Polly realised she was in for the Spanish Inquisition.

The journey took about thirty minutes and her mother must have said, 'How are you going to tell poor Gregg?' at least three times in quick succession. But Polly didn't answer.

Two hours later she was in Orthapaedic theatre having surgery on her leg. Fortunately her ribs and spinal column were only bruised and there appeared to be no long-term damage.

After the procedure, she was transferred to a private room. She was tucked up in her bed with her leg in traction when her father entered the room.

'This has been the worst day of my life Polly. You've always been a joy to your mum and I, and I genuinely felt a lot of love and affection for Spartan. But here I stand and I feel that I have lost you both on the same day. How could you do this to Gregg? The Registrar told me that your baby was unharmed. How long have you been seeing that Spanish gigolo?'

Polly didn't answer. All she knew was that being with Hector had made her realize she did not love Gregg. 'I'm really tired dad. Can I talk to you and mum about it when we're at home?'

Her father agreed and left. She was on her own at last, and could not stop the tears flowing when she thought about Spartan. He'd been like a brother, sharing a great adventure with her. Her mind flashed back to that last ride and how she'd felt something was wrong. She couldn't shake the feeling that foul play had taken place.

Eventually she dozed off only to be woken by a light kiss on her forehead. Hector stood by her bed with a massive bouquet of flowers in his arms. He bent toward her again and his lips found hers. She accepted the first kiss but put her hands out to push him away before he could break down all her barriers again.

He pulled up a chair and asked her how she was and how long it would be before she would be able to leave the hospital. She told him that the surgeon said she could leave hospital tomorrow but that it would be six weeks before she could have the plaster off her leg and she'd need a further six months of physiotherapy before she'd be able to walk properly and ride again.

Hector stayed for another hour and they talked. Hector told her that he lived up in the mountains in Tenerife and had a large property business there and in Southern Spain. Riding was his passion and he had built a stables complex next to the house with some twenty horses. 'You must come out and visit me as soon as your leg is better.'

It sounded like heaven to Polly. She didn't want to spoil things by telling him about the baby.

The following morning Polly's parents came to collect her. Her father showed her the 'Observer'. She was front-page news, for all the wrong reasons. She breathed a sigh of relief that there was no mention or pictorial evidence of Hector.

Once they were home Polly's mother made tea. Polly sat down and her mum spoke. 'Your father and I couldn't sleep last night. We were so shocked by the events of the day, but the one thing we agreed on was our unconditional love for you Polly .We will support you, whatever your decision is with regards to the baby.'

Her father chipped in. 'It might be good for us to hear the patter of tiny feet again around the house. It would help us all get over what has happened to Spartan.'

'Dad, I haven't decided whether I'll keep the baby.'

'Whatever you do is alright by us poppet.'

'Would you mind if I go to my room? I need to ring Gregg.'

'It's not too late for you to stay together is it?' said her mum.

'It would be wrong to deceive him about the baby and I've come to realise it was fondness not love that I felt for him.'

Polly dreaded her call to Gregg. His face appeared on the screen of her laptop and her heart sank. He smiled broadly at her. 'Great news Poll! I'll be back home in ten days, so get that hotel booked.'

'I've just had the worst weekend of my life Gregg.' Said Polly and she proceeded to tell him about Spartan's death and her injuries.

'While I was lying alone in the hospital I realised that I'm not ready for marriage. I think the world of you, but I'm not the right person to be your wife and the mother of your children.'

'Where did all of this come from?' said Gregg, aghast. 'At least let me come and take you for dinner when I get back, and we can talk things through properly.'

Polly agreed, even though she thought it would be like slow torture.

That afternoon the phone rang. There was a knock on her bedroom door and her father held the phone out to her. 'It's Hector for you.'

'Hello Hector'

'There's been a change of plan for this evening my darling. If you can manage it, I'll take you to my hotel for a meal and have you home and tucked up in bed by eleven thirty.'

Polly made sure she was ready for him, leaning on her crutches at the front door when he arrived to pick her up.

'I cannot believe how beautiful you look my darling, I'm so jealous of those crutches.'

Polly slid carefully into the front seat of his Mercedes and he laid the crutches on the back seat. They had an enjoyable meal at Hector's hotel restaurant and sat in the lounge afterward having liqueurs and coffee. Polly couldn't stop herself from looking at his face and the dark pools of his eyes. She ached to go to bed with him, but her physical condition was an insurmountable impediment.

'Time to get you home.' came the dreaded words.
They set off and it wasn't long before Polly realised they were not headed back to her parents' house.

Hector turned the Mercedes into a dark, tree-shrouded layby, and brought the car to a halt. He looked at her with longing in his eyes. 'I want you Polly.'

Their lips entwined and their tongues flickered back and forth. He pulled down the zip on her dress, exposing her breasts and her swollen nipples.

'I can't Hector.' moaned Polly, but it did not stop him putting his hands up her dress and sliding her panties down over the plaster encasing her leg.

He left the driver's seat and came to her side of the car where he knelt between her spread legs. Then his head was between her thighs and he was working her with his tongue and his fingers. He was remorseless and she emitted a series of groans as her juices flowed. He stood up in front of her and that smile came again. 'Nice?'

Polly nodded her head.

'My turn now.' he said and stepped out of his trousers and underwear. His penis was erect and she knew what was coming. He pushed his fingers into her mouth and prised her lips apart. Her mouth formed an O as he slid his penis inside.

Polly had no experience of oral sex, but she followed Hector's instructions as he slid in and out of her, occasionally pushing further toward her throat. She heard him shout 'Faster! Faster!' until he withdrew suddenly and she felt his warm seed erupt over her naked breasts.

Then he kissed her again hard and she tasted her juices mixed with his fluid. After half an hour of slow petting he opened the door and went back to the driver's seat. It took her some time to rearrange her hair and her clothes but he reassured her that she looked as beautiful as ever.

She looked at her watch and gasped as she saw that it was one thirty. So much for the eleven thirty she'd told her father. They drove home silently. He opened the door for her, said 'I will ring you on Wednesday, my darling.' And was gone.

The front door opened before she reached it. Her father stood there with disappointed look on his face. He said nothing and turned away. She shuffled towards her room and collapsed on the bed.

The following week Polly returned to work. Many of her clients came and offered their solicitations and Mr. Wilson had the decency not to raise the sponsorship issue. Things were just about getting back to normal when Richard entered the bank and made a beeline for her desk. 'You need to take your coffee break now.' he said, urgently.

Ten minutes later they were in the Copper Kettle. 'The vet came to see me yesterday. They found traces of a tranquiliser in Spartan's blood. Not enough to knock him out but enough to make him woozy.' Said Richard.

Polly began to cry and told Richard how she had felt at the beginning of her round.

'I don't see how anyone could have administered it Polly. Spartan was guarded all the time he was at Hickstead.'

Polly told him about Caroline leaving the horse unguarded while she went to the loo.

'It's that bastard Pemberton!' said Richard.

'But Richard, we have no proof and we're not likely to get any. It's our word against his and he's far more powerful than us.'

Richard eventually calmed down and they agreed never to talk about the matter again.

Hector didn't make his promised phone call. Instead, the one she was dreading came on the Friday night. Gregg had arrived in the UK and was on his way home. He said he would call for her the following evening to take her for dinner.

As the next day dawned Polly went over and over in her mind what she was going to say, but she needn't have bothered. Her phone rang. It was Gregg.

'I'm not coming tonight. Rachel told me all about your behaviour. To think that I never once visited the brothels in Kabul. How could you do this Polly? I feel completely betrayed.'

Polly burst into tears, but all she could say was 'I'm so sorry Gregg. I didn't mean to hurt you.'

'Well you did. All our friends know about what a slut you are.'

She put the phone down, wiping tears from her face. That explained why she hadn't heard from Rachel or Caroline since the fall. It felt like her world had collapsed around her.

The following Polly arranged to take leave from work. She couldn't face the stares and the gossip. When her father asked why she wasn't going in she explained she wanted time to make a decision about the baby.

'Are you in love with Hector?'

'I don't really know what love is Dad. All I know is that when I'm with him I come alive.'

'Has he said how he feels about you?'

'No, and I'm afraid to ask him, I feel as if I don't know enough about him.'

'Let's have a family lunch on Sunday and talk everything through.'

The week passed slowly, with no visitors and no calls. She realized how things would be if she stayed in Midhurst.

On Sunday morning she helped her Mum prepare the meal. Her father opened a bottle of expensive red wine and set it on the table to breathe.

The front door bell rang and her father called out, 'Can you get that Polly?'

She almost fainted when she opened the door for there was Hector, immaculate in a navy blazer and cream slacks, and with a bunch of flowers in his hand.

Polly blushed. She hadn't bothered with make-up and was wearing a baggy old sweater and joggers.

'Your father says you have something to tell me.' said Hector said with a frown, as he pecked her on the cheek and edged past her into the living room.

Polly's mother suggested having a glass of wine on the patio before lunch and Hector followed her outside, as Polly grabbed her father's arm. 'What have you done!' she said, her eyes blazing.

'I simply did what I would have wanted had I been in his place. I told him how unhappy you were and he agreed to talk things through.'

They stepped out into the garden and Polly took a seat beside Hector while her father poured glasses of vintage Rioja.

'To the future!' Hector raised his glass and offered a toast before turning to Polly.

'We haven't known each other long, but I'm in love with you. Come back to Tenerife, live with me and let me be a loving father to our child.'

Polly could not stem her tears as Hector continued 'I'm sorry, but I can't marry you. My first wife is a Catholic.

We've been apart for seven years but she won't grant me a divorce.'

'It doesn't matter!' said Polly, wrapping her arms around him and holding him tight.

Dinner and the afternoon cemented a bond between Hector and her parents and he told them that they would be welcome guests at his villa. He returned to his hotel that night having first told Polly he would collect her late tomorrow morning and take her to the airport.

A new chapter in her life was about to begin.

Sunny Spain

The plane touched down in the early evening. Polly and Hector had spent the flight getting to know each other better. Hector asked her if she would agree to have their child brought up in the Catholic faith and Polly agreed. She asked if he had any children by his marriage and he shook his head.

He told her to take her time acclimatising and suggested she think about managing the stables project, and then he explained that he'd be away for periods of time, looking after his business interests on the European mainland. He told her that he company office and boardroom were part of the house and that his personal assistant Maria worked there.

On leaving the airport they were met by Hector's chauffeur.

'Good evening Gunther. This is Senorita Townsend. She'll be staying with us from now on.'

Gunther led the way to the car park where Hector's Range Rover was parked. Polly smiled when she noticed the personalised number plate.

Polly had never been to Tenerife before and was fascinated by the many small villages they passed through as the road climbed relentlessly. Hector explained that over ninety-five per cent of the population on the island was located along the coastline, most of it concentrated in the holiday resorts of Playa De Las Americas and Puerto De La Cruz, and the capital, Santa Cruz.

His house was located in a forested area, high in the mountains, half a mile from the main road to Mount Teide, where the air was much cooler. This made it more suitable for the training of horses.

They arrived at the entrance and a pair of ornate iron gates swung open to reveal a magnificent mansion at the end of a long driveway. 'What a beautiful house.' Said Polly

'Wait till you see it all,' he replied 'But first, it's time to meet your household.'

Gunther disappeared with their luggage and Hector guided Polly her into a grand hallway which was lit by a magnificent crystal chandelier.

Next to the staircase stood three women and two men. All but one of them sported smart uniforms monogrammed with the initials HS. Hector took Polly forward to be introduced. Rosa the chef and Elena the housemaid both curtseyed with beaming smiles. The two men bowed solemnly and were introduced as Sergio the handyman and Manuel the gardener.

The fifth person was Maria, Hector's assistant. She was young and stunningly attractive, with long black hair falling halfway down her back. She smiled and took Polly's hand. 'I'm so pleased to meet you Miss Townsend. Hector told me my first priority is to help you to choose a new wardrobe.'

Polly blushed. 'Thank you. I'm looking forward to getting to know you all, and to improving my Spanish.'

Hector smiled approval and led her towards a huge pair of patio doors at the rear of the hall. 'Let me show you the view before it goes completely dark.'

If the front of Hector's mansion was awesome, the rear left Polly lost for words. Beyond a lawned terrace, the ground fell away sharply and she could see for miles, all the way to the sea. There were clusters of lights dotted across the panoramic landscape.

To their right was a large meter infinity pool with a hydro pool and a Jacuzzi located on either side. Polly gasped with pleasure.

'I'm pleased you like it my darling, and I hope you agree it will be the perfect place to raise a family. Now let's go upstairs and get ready for dinner.'

Hector stooped and swung her into his arms. 'I believe this is a tradition when couples commit to each other.'

She met his smile as the staff applauded them. Upstairs, Hector carried her from room to room. She counted ten, at least. 'Plenty of room for nurseries.' he said, as he deposited her on the bed.

He gave her a soft kiss on her lips then said 'I'll leave you to freshen up.'

Polly's suitcases had been brought up to the room and she sorted out a summer dress that she thought would be appropriate and reasoned there would be plenty of time to unpack properly the following day. She undressed as quickly as she could and went for a shower, careful not to get her plaster wet.

She emerged to see Hector sitting naked on a chair beside the bed. He smiled slowly at her and said, 'You're so beautiful my wounded bird. Come here.'

He spun her round and lowered her gently onto his erect penis. She shuddered when he penetrated her. Taking her weight he slowly moved her up and down. It wasn't long before they came together, which necessitated a return journey to the shower, this time on a shared basis.

She felt as if she was glowing when Hector carried her back downstairs and placed her on one of the dining chairs. Dinner was a private event for them and featured freshly caught local fish as the main course. It was delicious. Polly said that she hadn't tasted anything like it before. Hector told her it was grouper.

Hector said he would be away on the mainland for two days but had given Maria instructions to take Polly shopping. 'Don't forget to spend plenty on lace underwear.' he said, looking into her eyes and sliding his hand up her dress.

When she awoke the next morning, Hector was gone. She dressed as quickly as she was able and with difficulty, made her way downstairs. Breakfast was served on the terrace under a brilliant blue sky. Maria was at the table, opposite Hector. With a smile, he set down his newspaper and rose to greet Polly.

She blushed when Maria asked if she'd slept well with a knowing smile. Hector told her he would take her for a tour of the stables after breakfast but then he would have to leave to catch his flight.

At the stables, Polly could see that no expense had been spared. There was an equine swimming pool, which was still under construction, and a rubber road that led from the horseboxes to the exercise paddocks, to prevent the five horses currently stabled there from jarring themselves.

Three of them were polo ponies, which Hector rode in competitions. There were also two retired thoroughbreds that he used for riding out. He told her to choose one of them as her own to ride it out as she wished. He planned to acquire further horses as the building work progressed.

Hector said goodbye with a lingering kiss and shortly before midday, Polly and Maria headed for their shopping trip in Santa Cruz, where they stopped for lunch at a boulevard café.

Maria asked a lot of questions and seemed disappointed about Polly's lack of experience with men. Over lunch, Polly asked Maria how long she'd worked for Hector.

'Five years. I often accompany him on business trips.' said Maria, with a look that hinted at, something, though Polly wasn't sure what. She let it go and the women headed for the shops, where Maria told her that Hector said she had an unlimited budget and that everything should be charged to his account.

After buying several formal gowns, and a variety of shoes Polly asked Maria if she'd mind leaving her for half an hour while she chose underwear. She was taken aback when Maria suggested she visit a sex shop in the adjacent street, where the selection would be more exotic.

After their purchases were complete, the women returned to the mansion where Polly asked about Hector's wife. 'An ice maiden who treated the staff as if they were something unpleasant on the sole of her shoe.' was the reply.

She went on to describe Hector's many girlfriends since he and his wife had separated and Polly was tempted to ask if she had left herself out.

They rounded off the two days by going for an excellent dinner at a renowned local tapas restaurant and Polly noted that there seemed to be a chemistry between Maria and the owner of the restaurant.

Hector returned the following day and they spent each morning that week going for rides along the paths in the forest. Once they bathed naked in a pool and made love afterwards, while their horses grazed contentedly.

The next six months passed quickly as Polly's pregnancy progressed. Her leg healed perfectly, though she stopped riding out at the six-month stage, as she was afraid of falling and harming her unborn child.

One night she and Hector were lying in each other's arms, basking in the afterglow of love making, when Hector asked her if she was happy and whether she missed her life with Spartan. She said that she felt guilty, because she rarely thought of him. One thing led to another and she ended up telling Hector about the events surrounding Spartan's death. A steely glare took over his eyes and he said times, 'He will pay. He will pay.'

Polly was kept busy, designing and supervising the finalisation of the stable complex and the installation of a small show jumping course in one of the adjoining paddocks. She had asked Hector if she could start a riding school after the baby was born and he readily agreed.

They had an English newspaper delivered each afternoon, which Polly read with her afternoon cup of tea. Shortly before the baby was due she noticed an article: 'Prominent Yorkshire businessman and equestrian killed in road accident.'

Bob Clifford-Pemberton had lost control of his BMW going around a tight bend and died when the car plunged down a ravine and burst into flames. Foul play was not suspected as the deceased was well over the legal limit for alcohol consumption. Remembering her recent conversation with Hector, Polly was initially unnerved, but put the events down to coincidence.

The birth happened when Hector was away on business but he returned home a quickly as possible to see mother and daughter, who the couple named Magdalena.

Polly's parents arrived shortly after the birth and stayed until the christening. Hector was a perfect host and Polly's father told everyone at dinner one evening that he'd never seen his daughter look so happy.

Not So Sunny Spain

From what Polly could see, the next seven years passed with no sign of an 'itch' on Hector's part. He remained an attentive husband and relished the new responsibilities of fatherhood.

Polly was happily settled in her new life, had become fluent in Spanish and taken out dual citizenship, and as for Magdalena, she was a jewel. At seven she was already an accomplished rider who loved her occasional trips to see her grandparents in England.

Polly devoted her life to her family's happiness, evidenced by the photographs littered around the house of special occasions like first steps, first length of the pool, plus numerous anniversary and birthday parties.

By now Polly was used to the regular business meetings that took place in Hector's office and had met most of his business associates. One afternoon she was about to telephone her mother when the office door burst open and two men stormed out.

'You will regret this Hector!' shouted one as he slammed the door behind him.

A screech of tyres and they were gone. Over dinner that evening Polly asked Hector what had happened. He told her that the two associates wanted him to sell his business to a third party, but he had refused.

He went on to tell her that it would be necessary for him to bring in some security for a while to guard the estate and that she should not go riding with Magdalena in the forest.

From now on, a bodyguard would accompany her whenever she left the estate to go shopping.

Despite her concerns, Polly adjusted to the new regime, even if she felt that she was now something of a prisoner in her own home.

Shortly afterwards she sat down to watch the evening news and was shocked by the lead story. The face of one of Hector's former business associates filled the screen above the headline 'Tenerife Time Share Tycoon Gunned Down'. She grabbed her phone and Hector's number, but without success.

When Hector arrived home the next morning she was about to ask him about the shooting, when the doorbell rang and Rosa appeared. 'Excuse me Senor Sanchez. Inspector

Ramirez of CNP is at the door and would like to ask you some questions.'

Leaving the room. Hector told Polly to stay where she was. She heard him invite the inspector into the office. After thirty minutes, Hector emerged with the policeman and told Polly had to go to Police Headquarters in Playa De Las Americas to continue the interview. His lawyer would meet him at the police station.

He returned that night at eleven, looking exhausted. No charges had been made against him, due to lack of evidence, but enquiries were continuing and his passport had been seized.

They sat up until the early hours of the morning talking and Hector told her more about his business. His company had a virtual monopoly on all timeshare developments in

Tenerife and he owned a massive portfolio of rental properties in Tenerife and mainland Spain, plus several casinos in mainland Europe.

Six months ago, he'd been approached by a group of Russians who had recently vacated a similar portfolio in Cyprus. They offered to buy his interests but at a significant amount below their market value. They left him with no illusions as to the risks he would run if he turned them down.

Hector was no stranger to working in this kind of environment and had strengthened his security arrangements. He would not answer when Polly asked him directly whether he had been involved in the murder, from which she drew her own conclusions.

They went to bed with an air of tension between them, something that had never existed before. This continued for several weeks until Hector came home one night and opened a bottle of champagne. 'I'm sorry to have put you through this my darling but I've reached a deal with the Russians and the war is over, and no charges will be brought against me.'

Polly sighed with relief and allowed him to take her in his arms. They made love for the first time in several weeks, though she still felt unsettled and unsure as to whether she'd been living a lie for the past seven years.

Spring came and with it a sense that normality had returned. They began riding out in the forest again, albeit with an armed security guard accompanying them.

Hector's trips abroad reduced and to her surprise, Polly found out she was pregnant again. They'd been trying without success since Magdalena was born. Polly decided she would not tell anyone until she was sure.

Things turned sour with the Russians when Hector found out they'd been trying to set up a drugs ring, selling to his tenants. He threw their board representatives out of the board meeting at which he produced the evidence. The tension was back again,

A week later, Polly went on her weekly shopping trip to Puerto De La Cruz. She stopped at her usual venue for lunch, had her meal and went to the rest room prior to departure. When she returned to her table, there was a large brown envelope on the seat, addressed to Senora Sanchez. She sat down and tore it open. The contents destroyed her life.

Inside were half a dozen coloured photographs, which showed Hector naked and indulging in a threesome with two women. Polly recognized one of the faces. It was Maria.

Never one to wallow in self-pity, Polly decided not to confront Hector but to fly back to England with Magdalena and start a new life there. She had sufficient money in her personal accounts to buy a small property and she should have no trouble finding a part time job.

Over the past year, Hector had destroyed the love she felt for him. He was probably a murderer and definitely a serial adulterer. She would keep the photographs somewhere safe should he ever try to take Magdalena and her new baby from her.

She began to make her preparations and travelled into Puerto De La Cruz to book flights for herself and Magdalena It only took thirty minutes to complete the booking and she set off back home with her security guard accompanying her in the car.

She realized something was wrong when she reached the entrance gates. They had been bulldozed. She accelerated towards the house. Her heart was in her mouth when she saw the two security guards lying, riddled with bullet holes on the ground outside. The front door was wide open. Polly raced inside, gulping for air as her chest tightened. Maria was slumped motionless in her chair in front of the office, with a single bullet wound in the centre of her forehead.

She burst into Hector's office and could not stop the tears. Hector was at his desk. Everything appeared normal until she noticed the red ring around his neck. He had been garroted.

There was only one thought on her mind. Magdalena. She shouted out her daughter's name but there was no reply.

Polly ran to the stairs and took them two at a time. She burst into Magdalena's room and felt as if her heart had stopped. Her daughter's body lay sprawled across the bed with a bloodstained pillow over her face. Polly gently removed the pillow and saw a single bullet wound in her daughter's forehead. She cradled Magdalena in her arms and climbed onto the bed beside to her. She sobbed violently. It felt as if her world had come to an end.

Downstairs she heard sirens as several police cars arrived, tyres skidding across the gravel. Inspector Ramirez rushed into the bedroom. He halted after he had taken in the scene. 'I am so sorry for your loss Senora Sanchez.'

Polly did not reply and continued rocking her daughter's body back and forth. 'I can assure you we will do everything we can to find the perpetrators of this atrocity. Europol's top investigators will arrive tomorrow to assist us with the investigation.'

It was two weeks before the bodies of Magdalena and Hector were returned. Polly's parent's arrived on the island. Then it was time for the funeral and she wept as the bodies of her daughter and lover were interred together. She did not tell her parents about Hector's indiscretions.

A week after the burial, Inspector Ramirez arrived with the head of the Interpol investigation. They wasted no time in telling her that they'd applied to the courts to sequester all of the property and cash assets owned by Hector Sanchez under the Proceeds of Crime legislation. They had evidence that Hector headed a major crime syndicate involved in property fraud, money laundering, trafficking and prostitution and advised her to get a good lawyer.

She had been in a daze since Magdalena's death and later that day she decided to go for a ride to try to clear her head, dismissing her bodyguard as she headed for the stables.

She was about three miles from the house when she heard the roar of an engine behind her. She turned around in the saddle and saw a black Range Rover racing towards her. A figure leaned out of the window with a sub machine gun in his hand, which he fired.

A bullet caught her horse on its quarter. It gave a loud whinny and reared up, unseating Polly. She hit the ground hard.

The car screeched to a halt and the gunman stepped out and walked slowly towards Polly, who lay helpless on the ground. He raised his gun when there was a sharp crack in the background and he fell like a stone to the ground. The Range Rover accelerated quickly and tore off, its passenger door gyrating wildly.

Polly could not raise herself upright. She had an agonizing pain at the bottom of her back. Her security guard, Michael came running up. 'Thank goodness you ignored my instructions.' croaked Polly.

Michael smiled and tried unsuccessfully to raise her to her feet. He flagged down an approaching car and explained what had happened. The driver rang emergency services and propped Polly's head up with a cushion, while Michael diverted traffic around the scene.

Polly awoke in a hospital bed the following day. She felt very drowsy, but recognised her father and mother sitting at the bottom of the bed. They pulled their chairs closer and stooped to kiss Polly on her forehead. Her father told her that a policeman was posted outside her door and that the doctor had arranged for her to have a body scan, as he was concerned about the damage to her back, which appeared to have aggravated the problems she suffered after her fall at Hickstead.

That afternoon Inspector Ramirez visited her with his Interpol colleague. They asked her again whether she had any knowledge of her husband's business affairs and accepted her negative reply. He told her they had swooped on the headquarters of a Russian crime syndicate near Los Cristianos and made a number of arrests. He could not be sure, but he thought her life was no longer in danger.

He went on to tell her that the house was to be seized along with Hector's other assets and he regretted that she would have to vacate it one week after she returned from hospital. Scans revealed she would need a major operation on the lower part of her back.

Her father's view was that she should have her operation in Spain. Afterwards she should fly back to the UK to have her baby.

Three months later her migration was complete and she alighted from the Tenerife flight at Gatwick and headed back to Midhurst. She had received a massive bonus when Hector's lawyer came to see her in hospital and told her that he'd worked out a deal with the police. The value of Hector's assets seized was some fifty million euros and he had argued successfully that a retention of five million by the estate would be good value if the seizure was not contested.

The lawyer told Polly that there was no likelihood that anyone would challenge her status as sole heir. She wondered what life would be like as a wealthy widow.

PART 3

BEKI'S STORY

Family Life

The sun had just begun to cast its light through the wicker walls of the house on the Ethiopian plain. Beki rolled silently out of the bed she shared with her two younger sisters and tried not to wake them. She woke her older brother, Sami, as he had to set off for his job as a labourer on one of the neighbouring farms.

She looked in on her mother to see if there was anything she needed. The rasping breaths were an indication that her mother did not have long left to live. She had suffered from AIDS for three years and could no longer work nor support her family. Their father had died five years ago of the same cause. It was up to ten-year-old Beki and twelve-year-old Sami now. They received a small amount of financial help from a charity, SOS, which supplemented Sami's meager wage and prevented them from starving.

Beki slipped into her dress, which had seen better days, and splashed some water on her face. She picked up the water carrier and stepped outside.

The small village was bathed in early morning light. Beki strapped the water carrier onto her frail shoulders and set off on her daily journey to Lake Hawassa.

She broke into a trot and it was not long before she had found her a rhythm. By making her journey at first light she could return before the daily temperature reached its fifty-degree peak, and if she was lucky, she'd finish her chores in time to catch the school bus to Hawassa. If not, she had another three mile run on her hands.

She arrived at the water purifying station and as usual was first in the queue. The water controller, Mwombi, smiled at her. 'How is my little antelope this morning?'

'Fine Mwombi. How is the water level?'

'Good this year. There must have been more rain in the mountains last winter. Hand me your containers.'

Beki passed them over and he filled them to three quarter level. No point in going any further as the precious liquid would be spilled on the way home. Mwombi helped Beki to hoist the carrier onto her shoulders 'How is your mother?' he asked.

'I don't think she has long left.'

Mwombi shook his head slowly.

The return journey was a test of endurance that Beki had carried out every day for the last three years, since her mother became too ill to fetch the water herself.

Eventually she reached home and got changed for school. She cooked a gruel breakfast for her sisters and made sure they looked presentable before they joined her on the school bus. Finally she took her mother her breakfast and sat with her for five minutes.

Her mother tried to have a conversation about school but was soon racked with violent coughing and turned to the wall with tears in her eyes.

The bus was full, but Beki's friend Bela had kept her a seat on the clapped out lorry that chugged its way around the villages surrounding Hawassa every morning and evening.

The school was a relatively modern building funded by SOS. The headmistress was Madame Bouchard, a French-Canadian woman in her mid fifties. Her two support teachers were both former pupils who had gone to college in Addis Ababa.

Lessons began at nine-thirty. The children learned English and basic arithmetic, plus art, music and drama. Any pupil who showed special abilities was given extra tuition, with a view to gaining entry at one of the country's further education colleges.

When Beki and her companions arrived at school there was a ball game in progress. 'Here come the Bedouins!' came a voice from a group of better-dressed children who stood together at the centre of the playground.

Beki and her friends ignored the taunt and carried on walking, but an older girl stepped forward and said, 'Where are your camels? You all smell of camel dung!'

Beki ignored that taunt too and led her group to the corner of the yard. The girl followed them, grabbed hold of Beki's shoulder and spun her round. She had her hand raised to strike when a voice came from the school entrance. 'Line up! Line up!'

It was Madame Bouchard, who taught the older children. As everyone formed lines the girl the big girl snarled at Beki. 'I'll get you tonight after school.'

The day passed quickly. First lessons, then lunch, which was often the only meal many of the children got to eat all day. As soon as the bell for end of day rang, Beki decided to grab her things and run for the bus, but as she ran round the corner of the building she found the bully and her gang waiting for her.

'Well, if it isn't camel dung girl.' said her tormentor. 'Time for you to grovel in front of your betters.'

The girl pushed Beki violently. She staggered backwards but remained on her feet. The girl pushed her again.

By this time several of the children who caught the bus had appeared. 'Leave her alone you bully!' shouted Bela, which elicited a swift reply.

'You're next, Bedouin lover.'

The bully tried to slap Beki, but the younger girl began to move her feet quickly, like the character in her favourite film, 'Karate Kid'. She dodged the girl's clumsy attempts to punch her. By now quite a crowd had gathered and most of them were cheering Beki on, much to the frustration of her opponent who grew increasingly desperate.

She launched a charge at Beki, head down and a murderous look in her eye. In one movement, Beki sidestepped, jumped and scissor kicked her opponent on the side of her head. The girl went down as if pole-axed. All of that running barefoot had hardened the skin on Beki's feet.

The crowd went silent, then an almighty cheer followed and her fellow travellers picked Beki up and carried her above their heads to the bus cheering.

After this incident Beki and her friends had no more trouble from school bullies, though she received a stern telling off from Madame Bouchard the following day. Once Beki left her office, a slow smile spread over the head teacher's face.

One morning, as Beki returned from the lake, she saw the doctor's jeep parked outside their hut. She put the buckets down and ran inside but it was too late. Her mother's body lay beneath a blanket, and her siblings were huddled together with tears streaming down their faces.

Running Into The Spotlight

After their mother died, SOS stepped in to find someone to take care of the children. And so Niobe came into their lives. She was from a neighbouring village and had lost her own children to malaria.

Niobe was a cheerful woman who adapted to her new role well. Since losing her family she'd rented a house in Hawassa and took Beki and her sisters to live with her there. Sami moved out to the farm where he worked and only returned home on Sundays. Niobe made sure that meals were extra special when he was back and the siblings were together again for a few precious hours

Life was easier in Hawassa. There was no need for Beki to make her water journeys and the children soon found friends and playmates. After a while, Beki found she missed her daily journey and her chats with Mwombi in the shade of the pumping house, so once a week she took long runs out to the lake and back. Once became twice and soon she made the run every day, except Sunday.

Beki worked hard at her lessons too, and Madame Bouchard realised she had an exceptional pupil on her hands. She loaned Beki some of her own books and was amazed at the speed they were returned.

Not long after her twelfth birthday, Madame Bouchard called Beki to her office. There was a regional schools' athletics meeting in Hawassa and she'd been invited to send a small team. She asked Beki if she would like to represent the school in the one-mile race. Beki's friend Bela would also be on the team.

Beki was excited by this news and trained extra hard. She told Mwombi and he marked out a one-mile track, timing her laps with a stopwatch.

At their first training session Mwombi slumped to the ground in shock. Beki had run the mile over unbroken ground in four minutes and fifteen seconds, and that after running seven miles to get to the track!

Over the next month, Beki's cut this to four minutes ten seconds, and the week before the regional meeting Mwombi visited Madame Bouchard and told her to make sure as many of the school and Beki's family attended as possible.

The day arrived and there was huge excitement in the school. Madame Bouchard provided shorts and tops emblazoned with the school logo and offered to buy the runners spiked shoes, but Beki declined. She preferred to run barefoot.

There was a huge crowd around the track in Hawassa, a mixture of children and parents from participating schools, a few reporters and representatives from the Ethiopian Athletics Association.

The day began with the one-hundred-metre race and Bela finished third. She came second in the long jump to rapturous applause from her schoolmates.

The mile was the Blue Riband event and fourteen athletes lined up on the start line. There was a fair bit of jostling and Beki found herself behind the front row. Then the starting pistol fired and they were off. .

Beki only knew one way to run and that was as fast as possible. After two hundred metres she'd raced past the rest of the field and into a clear lead. One of the national coaches gasped when logged the time at the end of the first lap. Fifty-eight seconds!

By the end of the second lap Beki was a clear hundred metres in the lead and seemed full of energy as she glided over the surface of the track like an antelope. By the end of the third lap the crowd were bellowing at the tops of their voices. 'Go Beki! Go!'

In the home strait Beki tired but crossed the line with a time of four minutes and seven seconds, a time that would have won the senior women's trials.

The national coach turned to Madame Bouchard and asked 'Where have you been hiding this girl? In twenty years as an athletics coach I've never seen anything like it.'

'That's nothing. Wait until you see her run ten thousand metres!' said Mwombi.

Beki had barely got her breath back when she was surrounded by a mass of clapping children and adults. The reporters were not far behind and there was a cacophony of clicking cameras as she held aloft the trophy. The chief reporter asked if she was surprised ay her result.
'I don't know. I just let my legs run. Sometimes I feel as if the wind is in my heart. Today I kept thinking that my mama was looking down on me and I ran my fastest for her.'

At school the following day more journalists arrived to interview Beki. A TV crew arrived to film her at home with her family. It wasn't long before a delegation from the Ethiopian Athletics Association held a meeting with Madame Bouchard, Niobe and Beki. They wanted Beki to come and train with them full time in Addis Ababa. A college education for Beki would be provided and she would stay with a respected family in the city.

Beki couldn't visualize living anywhere else but Hawassa. She would miss her daily runs to Lake Hawassa. Madame Bouchard explained to Beki what an amazing opportunity she had. Yes, it would take time to get used to life in the city life would be like in the city, but she should consider her future.

It was agreed that Beki would leave at the end of the current term. She went to see Mwombi and told him she would send him the first medal she won, and the pair said a tearful goodbye.

An official from the Athletics Association arrived to escort Beki. En route to Addis Ababa they stopped at McDonalds for lunch. Beki was wide eyed when confronted with fast food and a milk shake but made short work of them. She would have plenty to tell her sisters when she wrote to them.

The city streets were like racetracks with all types of vehicles hurtling along. Eventually Beki and her escort arrived outside a large house on a tree-lined street.

The door swung open to reveal a tall man with silver hair. Standing next to him was a plump woman with a kind face and sparkling eyes. 'Welcome to our home child. I am Pastor Fanduli and this is my wife, Mavona.'

Beki greeted them shyly. Then Mavona led her upstairs to her room. Beki had never seen such luxury. At home she usually slept on the floor beside her sisters.

After Mavona left Beki kicked off her shoes and lay back on the bed. It was so soft. She bounced up and down, giggling. Then she washed and put on the dress and shoes Madame Bouchard had given h She looked at herself in the full-length mirror and twirled around, admiring her reflection.

After the Fanduli's gave her a tour of the house and garden she was led to the dining room and pointed toward a seat opposite Mavona's, where an array of knives, forks and spoons was laid out on a fine linen table mat. Mavona could see the confusion on Beki's face and explained the purpose of each piece of cutlery.

Beki had to fight off drowsiness during dinner. She was exhausted by everything that had happened that day, and as soon as she could she said good night and made her way upstairs. She was so tired that she fell asleep straight away although she could not bring herself to put her head on the pillow, which seemed a very strange object indeed.

City Life

After breakfast the following morning, Mavona took Beki to the city centre on a shopping trip. Beki had never seen so many people in one place and could not help being nervous when they had to cross the roads in front of all those speeding cars. After buying school uniform they stopped for lunch at a busy restaurant where the noise of so many chattering people made Beki's head ache. She was quiet in the taxi home and went to bed early that night.

The next day, she woke to bright sunlight and dressed in her new uniform. The crisp blouse felt strange against her skin, and the skirt made her legs itch.

Mavona came with her to St Margaret's College. They travelled on the bus Beki would need to catch each morning. The Headmistress was called Madame Penoir. She welcomed Beki with a smile and told her the college was extremely proud of its record in athletics.

Madame Penoir was impressed by Beki's breadth of reading. However mathematics was a different matter. It was clear Beki was at least a year behind her age group.

Beki said she was prepared to work hard to make up the lost ground. Then it was time for classes to begin. As well as the usual subjects, there were games lessons on Tuesdays and Thursdays and the athletics club met twice a week after school. The national coach arranged for Beki to have a personal trainer who would work with her on the other evenings and on Saturday mornings.

Beki was awe-struck at her first session with the national distance-running coach, Taresh Nkoumi, but she soon relaxed and enjoyed learning a series of warm-up exercises that would loosen her body before each run.

At their next session Taresh taught her how to breathe properly and it was lesson four before Taresh any work was done on the track, and Beki was finally able to show her coach what she could do.

Over the next few weeks Taresh realised she had a future world champion on her hands. It was decided Beki would run in the National Junior championships, which were two months away.

Beki was homesick so Mavona arranged for a visit back to her village. When she arrived her old classmates waved greeted her with flags and cries of 'Welcome home Beki!'

She waved joyously and went forward to hug her sisters and Niobe and to shake hands with Madame Bouchard. Bela ran up and told her she too had qualified to attend Beki's school in the city. Beki was thrilled to know her friend would soon be joining her

Three days passed quickly and on the first morning she ran out to the lake to see Mwombi. She brought him one of Niobe's homemade cakes that he sliced and put onto plates, while she told him about the National Championships that were coming up. He said he would be there to cheer her on.

Beki arrived back in Addis Ababa for the start of school term and soon fitted back into her routine. The weeks passed and soon it was time for Championships to begin. Beki arrived at the stadium with Taresh. They walked around the track together and Taresh told Beki to visualize herself running clear of the field and breasting the finishing tape.

There were twelve runners in the eight hundred metres event. In qualifying, Beki recorded a time that was five seconds faster than any of the other runners.

As the girls lined up on the start line, the announcer could not contain the excitement in his voice as he announced to the crowd that they might well see something special that day.

The race began and Beki sprinted straight into the lead and was twenty metres clear at the end of the first lap, which she had run in a staggering fifty two seconds.

As she rounded the final bend the crowd chanted her name as one. Beki breasted the tape in one minute and fifty-nine seconds. Officials huddled together and then the announcement came. 'You've all been privileged to see the junior world record for eight hundred metres broken by a thirteen year old Ethiopian girl.'

Reporters immediately surrounded Beki but she ignored them and jogged through the crowd to hug her waiting family and friends.

The following day the crowd was even larger, and there were television vans from both national and international stations.

When the twelve runners lined up for the start of the mile race, there was a hush of anticipation. The starting pistol cracked and Beki set off at her usual fast pace, but last year's winner kept pace. The tall girl bumped Beki on purpose. Beki refused to be intimidated but at the first bend the girl leaned in hard on her forcing her to lose her stride.

Beki dropped back a couple of yards and collected her thoughts. Her opponent moved out a lane as if daring Beki to run up her inside. Beki accepted the challenge and accelerated up the inside as they approached the bend. She heard the girl breathing heavily. She mouthed insults as Beki drew level, and then leaned over violently in an attempt to knock Beki off the track. Beki slowed and the girl's attempt failed. Instead she went tumbling to the ground as Beki picked up the pace and ran on to reclaim the lead.

She was almost twenty metres ahead of the field and crossed the line in a time of four minutes and three seconds winning another junior world record. The applause went on for at least ten minutes, and Beki's assailant slunk away in disgrace.

It seemed as if half of Addis Ababa was there on the final day of the championships to watch Beki run her first five thousand metre race which she won with ease, while the crowd roared her name and she sprinted round the final lap to add a third world record to her list of achievement.

By now Beki's performance had drawn the attention of several international TV stations and it wasn't long before she was offered a two million dollar sponsorship deal with Nike. This was money beyond her wildest dreams. She could anything, go anywhere. It was a miracle.

Bela arrived in the city and she and Beki were as inseparable as ever. They often trained together and enjoyed trips to the cinema, where Beki paid for the best seats in the house. Both girls were excited when they were selected to represent their country in the Junior World Championships, which would be help in Paris.

The girls could not stop talking about the trip and spent hours on the internet looking at places of interest, fashion and the music and arts scene.

The crowd for the National Athletics Championships was twice the normal size. Everyone had come to see the new 'Wonder Girl' of athletics. With her small frame, Beki was half the size of some of her opponents in the mile race.

The gun cracked and they were off. Beki took the lead as usual, but was closely tracked by three other athletes, all of whom travelled easily. But Beki held them off and the last lap was a classic with the crowd roaring Beki on throughout.

Her time was announced and the cheers became louder. Three minutes and fifty-two seconds, just two seconds outside the world record and the second fastest women's mile race ever.

With that, Beki became the new poster girl of world athletics. She was thrilled when Bela finished runner up in the long jump.

The summer passed in a whirl and as an investment, Beki bought a luxurious town house with a swimming pool in Addis Ababa. More sponsorship deals came with a fashion brand and an advert for Coca Cola. Several boys tried their luck on weekend shopping trips to the City Mall but Beki declined politely as she did not feel any attraction for them.

Then it was time to leave for Paris. The two girls were stunned by their first class flight to Charles De Gaulle airport. Madame Bouchard even permitted them to have a small glass of champagne and orange juice and several passengers and members of the crew asked for Beki's autograph.

On arrival, the first thing that struck Beki was the temperature. It was late summer in France but it was some twenty degrees cooler than the girls were used to in Ethiopia.

In the two weeks before the championships, the girls visited all the usual tourist attractions. They marvelled at The Eiffel Tower, The Louvre, Versailles and Fontainebleau, followed everywhere by the press. Beki proved to be a natural on camera and the world was soon familiar with her beaming, open smile.

The championships began and under Taresh's close supervision, Beki spent twice the amount of time warming up for the fifteen hundred metre race, which turned out to be something of a procession and Beki did not come anywhere near her winning time from the Ethiopian National Championships.

The five and ten thousand metre races were a different kettle of fish. Three Kenyans qualified for each final and during the five thousand metres they got around Beki and jostled her throughout the first half of the race, until she was in fourth position with two laps to go. But she ran a staggering final eight hundred metres and came home in the lead. The crowd erupted in cheers when she stepped up to collect the gold medal.

In the ten thousand metres, the Kenyans ran close to her. One of their runners cut in sharply in front, causing Beki to slow. She felt a sharp pain, looked down and saw blood trickling down her leg. She had been spiked. Ignoring the pain she pulled to the outside and put in a one-mile burst of four minutes and twenty seconds, which put her way out in front. Again, she won the race.

Womanhood

After Beki's fifteenth birthday she and Taresh talked through the annual calendar. Beki said she would like to try marathon running but decided to wait until after she had competed in the Olympics. Instead, Taresh suggested she take part in the Las Vegas and Rome Grand Prix events.

She was thrilled by the news and couldn't wait to tell Bela. But Bela didn't seem excited which was strange. Both girls studied hard for the first stage of their school certificates and Bela became more and more withdrawn.

The truth came out one night when they were testing each other on geography. Beki teased Bela about the size of her breasts and Bela burst into tears.

When she'd arrived home from Paris she'd felt as though someone was watching her whenever she took a shower at home. Then one afternoon the shower curtain was pulled back by her guardian Mr. Akani, who stood there naked. She cowered against the wall but he told her not to be frightened. He took the sponge from her and began to wash her all over, telling her how beautiful she was and that he loved her. He asked her to hold his erect penis and work it in her hand. It wasn't long before he came, spraying her stomach with his hot seed.

Bela was too afraid to tell anyone and Mr. Akani continued to molest her, eventually raping her one afternoon when his wife was out. These assaults continued until the inevitable happened. Two months before the national championships, Bela discovered she was pregnant.

Beki was shocked but determined to help her best friend as much as she could. It was a good job Bela also had a sponsorship deal with Nike. Niobe agreed to look after the baby once it was born, and Bela moved back to the village.

Beki confronted Bela's tormentor at a Board meeting of the National Athletics Association and told him that unless he resigned immediately, she would tell the media about his actions.

Bela went on to have a healthy baby girl. She moved back to Addis Ababa a year later and resumed her academic and athletic careers, as well as her friendship with Beki.

The following year Beki travelled back east. She'd thought Paris was cold, but Moscow was positively freezing and she kept herself well wrapped up in the two weeks lead in to the

Championships, where all her races were bloodless victories.

Then it was on to Las Vegas. Beki was awestruck by the city and marveled at the huge hotels and bright shopping malls.

The day of the Grand Prix arrived and Beki had just completed her warm up exercises when a young black man came up to her. Beki looked up. He was very handsome and she blushed as he sat down beside her.

'You're Beki, aren't you? My name is Kobe Johnson and I'm part of the USA relay team.'

The next ten minutes went by in a flash as they found out about each other. Beki had never felt physical attraction before and found the warm feeling growing inside her somewhat confusing.

Kobe asked if he could meet her after the event and take her for a meal and then dancing. Beki said she would have to get Taresh's permission first but she would definitely meet him back at the hotel for a coffee.

But Taresh told Beki that she should be focused on the race, rather than going on a date. Eventually she promised that Beki could meet Kobe if she won her race, but she should be back in her room by midnight.

Beki won her race with ease.

That night, Kobe waited for her in the lobby of her hotel. He looked amazing, in tight white jeans and a navy blue top.

They enjoyed dinner at a cosy Italian restaurant and then they were on the dance floor at the nightclub in Bellagio's, where Kobe proved himself to be an expert. Then they went to Beki's hotel for a final coffee.

During the evening she found out that Kobe came from Washington and was in his first year studying law at Princeton University. He had two older brothers and a younger sister. Beki explained that this was her first ever date and asked him if he had a girlfriend. He said he was currently single. The evening ended with Beki promising to meet Kobe again when they got to Rome for the next athletics event in their packed schedule.

The following morning she called Bela and told her she had a boyfriend. She felt as if she wanted to tell the world. Then it was time to pack and leave for the airport.

In Rome, Kobe and Beki spent every spare hour together, holding hands as they wandered through the streets of the beautiful city, until the night Beki invited Kobe back to her room.

It was the best night of Beki's life. The young athletes undressed each other slowly. Kobe was a gentle lover and brought her to a climax before he entered her. Eventually the couple fell exhausted into each other's arms and slept.

The following day was taken up with race after race and the lovers only found time for a brief kiss outside the dressing room. Beki was her usual peerless self, winning her race by thirty metres.

Back in the hotel she was about to take a shower when the telephone rang. It was Kobe. He was feeling down after losing his race and said he wanted to be alone, but agreed to meet her for breakfast so they could spend their last day in Rome together.

Morning came and Kobe was twenty minutes late. He looked dreadful. His eyes were bloodshot and his hair was unkempt.

He ordered a pot of strong black coffee. Beki tried to cheer him up and took his hand. A feeling of panic grew in her stomach when she saw that he could not bring himself to look her in the eye. Then the bombshell came. He said that he'd let her down. He had gone out on the town last night with two of his teammates and he had joined them in snorting cocaine. After a drunken brawl, he and his friends had been arrested. Their Team Manager was so incensed he had booked them on a flight home that afternoon.

With tears in her eyes Beki said goodbye and spent the rest of her day in her room. The newspapers arrived and she read an article about the events of the previous night, shocked to discover that the young Americans had been arrested outside a well-known brothel.

Taresh told Beki that she'd learned her first lesson in love and she resolved never to let her guard down with a man until she knew him well. She felt small and stupid as she packed for the long trip home to Addis Ababa.

Many A Slip

Once back home, Beki spent the winter training. She often met Bela and the two decided they would live together in Beki's house in Addis Ababa. Bela was keen to resume her athletics career but it would be more difficult with a child to care for.

Christmas came and Beki's brother announced his engagement. The wedding would take place the following month.

Beki remembered how Samuel had kept the family going by laboring long hours on neighbouring farms when still only a child himself. She invited him and his heavily pregnant fiancée to dinner and told them she had bought Samuel a farm where the couple could live and bring up their family. The young lovers wept with joy.

Then the season began and Beki was off to the airport again, this time to compete in a cross-country event in Belgium. Her main concern was the cold weather and for the first time she wore shoes and to avoid slipping on the muddy ground.

Beki loved cross-country. She felt as free as a bird and smashed the world record, crossing the line over two hundred metres in front of her nearest rival.

The World Championships came next, on an established course over England's West Sussex downs, where the ground was sodden due to weeks of heavy rain.

After less than a mile, Beki was out on her own some fifty metres clear of the field. The course comprised two four kilometer laps and Beki was over one hundred meters ahead as she began the second slow climb through the forest, followed by a fast descent and a half mile flat run to the finish line.

She passed a thick copse when a group of wood pigeons took flight with a rush of wings. . Beki was startled and lost her footing. She skidded at high speed into a large boulder beside the track and the crack as her leg shattered could be heard one hundred yards away.

Beki was in agony for twenty minutes, until a team of paramedics arrived and stretchered her to a waiting ambulance.

X-rays revealed she'd sustained a double fracture of her right leg. The prognosis was not good. Her Olympic dream was over.

It was so ironic that after all these years running barefoot, she had sustained a major injury on only her second ever run in trainers.

PART 4

SELMA'S STORY

Armageddon

'Putain!'

Selma swore as she kicked the Coke machine for the fourth time, but it refused to give up its contents. At the end of a fourteen-hour shift she was in desperate need of liquid. It was sweltering in the basement of Aleppo's paediatric hospital, which stood in the eastern sector of the city. Money was tight since the start of the war and air conditioning was limited to the wards.

Two male orderlies were slumped on their seats some twenty yards away. One of them got up laughing at her as he did so. 'That's not how you do it Doctor. You have to treat the machine like a woman and give it plenty of foreplay before you ask it to give out.'

He smiled at her and held his hand out for her coin. She handed it over blushing profusely and ten seconds later the delivery had taken place.

Selma took the can and walked back to her office. She had some paperwork to finish and then she was off for four days. She was really looking forward to spending a few days with her family, starting with a long sleep in her own bed.

She finished off the Pharmacy Requisition Form for the following week and left it in her out-tray. Despite the war supplies were still reliable as there were multiple routes open out of the city.

It was essential for all citizens to carry their identity papers, which they could be asked to produce by different factions several times on a single journey.

On the frontline, atrocities were commonplace, however family life had been subject to minimal disturbance for the citizens of East Aleppo.

Selma had her own car, which was emblazoned with a red caduceus, the sign of her profession. She picked up her allocated escort at the barracks just inside the hospital gates. It was three in the morning when she made it home and she crept upstairs without disturbing anyone, changed into her cool cotton pyjamas and was soon fast asleep.

She rose late the next morning and joined her family for one of their regular brunches. As usual her father, Hamid, sat at the head of the table. He was Professor of Medicine at the

Al Daquaaa hospital and head of the medical committee that organised the provision of medical services in rebel held territory. He'd been so proud when Selma returned to Syria earlier that year, having obtained her doctorate at the University of Boston.

Selma's older brother Hassan sat beside his father. Hassan had trained as a lawyer but now served as a colonel in the Free Syrian Army. Selma's two younger sisters, Sonia and Yasmin, were still at school.

Hamid blessed the food and welcomed Selma and Hassan to the table. As they ate the family discussed rumours of proposed Russian involvement in the war. Some said Putin's forces would soon launch a major air and ground assault.

If the rumours were true, there'd be a big increase in casualties. Hamid asked Selma if she would consider joining his surgical unit.

She was honoured by her father's request, as it meant she would be the only practicing female surgeon in Syria
The rumoured assault began three months later with a massive airstrike. Selma would never forget that day, a day of continuous sirens and broken bodies.

For three days Selma worked around the clock, snatching a few minutes' sleep wherever she could and alternating between surgical and triage duties. She was no stranger to the horrors of war but the sheer scale of the injuries, particularly those to young children, tested her professional resolve.

When she eventually emerged from the hospital into the light of day, she was horrified at the scene in front of her. A pall of grey dust hung in the air and drifted between piles of rubble, which had once been houses and shops.

Her driver reassured told her that her parents' house had not been hit. However he told her that she must pick up a safety helmet and said the journey from the hospital was likely to take twice as long as usual, as the roads had been so badly damaged.

Al Qaeda units now manned several checkpoints and she watched in horror as a man was brutally beaten, right in front of her vehicle.

She breathed a sigh of relief when she was dropped off in front of her parent's house. Several houses on the block had been hit and demonstrated no signs of life. Her mother beckoned her to follow her down to the cellar when she entered the house. She had divided the living space into a family and eating room and a sleeping room, which contained five single beds.

'The shower room is still working upstairs if you would like to freshen up. Then I suggest you get some sleep and we can have a family meal tomorrow.'

That sounded good to Selma who was exhausted. She had to be wakened by Yasmin in the morning to join the family for lunch. She looked in the mirror in the bathroom and reflected on how life had changed for her family and hundreds like them in the city. How long could they last?

The meal took its usual format and in many ways resembled a corporate boardroom. Selma's father spoke first and said that rebel-held Aleppo was in a desperate battle for survival and would have fallen already if it had not been for the supporting US airstrikes which held the government ground forces at bay. The arrival of more and more Al Qaeda units gave them a chance and kept supply routes open. However more and better artillery was of critical importance and there was little or no chance of victory, which had seemed a realistic possibility two years ago. Over twenty five per cent of the population had been killed or had fled toward the refugee camps.

Hassan asked if they should be prepared to leave. He was worried what life would become with Al Qaeda controlling more and more of the city's defences and everyday life too. There seemed little accountability within their command structure.

Selma said that she could not abandon the hospital, which stood between life and death for thousands of citizens, particularly young children. However, her mother pointed out that there were already far more Syrians living in the refugee camps than remained in Aleppo, and her services as a doctor would be just as valuable there.

Selma's mother had increasingly worried about the welfare of her younger daughters who were at risk not only from injury from air strikes but assault from their so-called 'protectors'. Several young women whose parents had been killed in air strikes had already been taken as 'comfort women' by the Al Qaeda units.

Flight

Her father said that ceasefire talks were scheduled for two weeks hence and they should postpone taking what would be the most important decision of their lives until then. In the meantime, he would try to arrange safe passage for them into Turkey and employment for them in medical and legal services there.

The next two weeks flew by, in Selma's case without any proper sleep. She tried not to reflect upon the number of death's that occurred on the wards due to wound infection, which had become more of a killer than impact wounds. She had become accustomed to acting as 'God' when managing the triage area after air raids had struck civilian areas.

Where possible, she tried to give priority to children and young adults who had greater life expectancy ahead of them and seemed better able to fight off infection than their elders. There was also a better chance of direct support from the many charities operating in Aleppo.

When she arrived back home the general consensus was that the ceasefire would not hold and was being used as an excuse by both sides to move troops and restock on arms. It was decided that they would abandon their house and make a run for the Turkish border in two weeks time.

Hassan said he would arrange for two large four-by-four vehicles, which they could stock up with essentials. He would drive his mother and the young girls. Selma would drive her father.

The departure date was brought forward by seven days after an incident the following week. Sonia and Yasmin were returning home from school as usual with their bodyguard, when they were stopped by a patrol of Al Qaeda fighters. These were different men to the patrol that normally guarded their parent's street.

The men began talking animatedly to the bodyguard and leering openly at the young girls. The bodyguard gesticulated and pointed out that they were under the direct protection of a colonel in the Free Syrian Army, however that seemed to make the situation worse, as several of the Al Qaeda spat at the mention of their so-called allies.

Out of the blue, one of the soldiers stepped up behind the bodyguard and knocked him unconscious. The girls screamed louder and louder as the soldiers dragged them towards a tent.

As soon as they were inside the soldiers told them to take their clothes off at knifepoint and they were passed from one to the other who fondled them and kissed their breasts while encouraging their colleagues to get the girls on the ground and hold their legs wide open.

The leader of the soldiers took his pants off and began to massage Yasmin's vagina while she continued to scream for help. Then, all hell was let loose.

The curtains were pulled back and four soldiers burst into the tent. Three wore the uniforms of the Free Syrian Army; the fourth wore an Al Qaeda captain's uniform. The leader of the would-be rapists started to get to his feet when the Captain shot him between the eyes. The other shoulders were bundled roughly outside and driven away in a jeep.

The Free Syrian Army contingent, who were led by Hassan, left the tent while the girls were told to get dressed and get into Hassan's vehicle. The Captain apologised to Hassan for the unacceptable behavior of his troops and said that the offenders would be put in the frontline of their next counter attack against government troops. Hassan thanked him for his help and drove the girls home where their mother comforted them.

It transpired that one of their neighbours had seen what was happening and had rung the girl's mother and she had rung Hassan immediately. All of the women were distressed and Hassan made them sit down and made them some strong coffee while he rang his father.

Hamid arrived home within fifteen minutes and hugged his wife and his daughter's tight. Hassan rang Selma and told her what had happened and she said she would return home that night at the end of her shift.

They talked through the night and planned their route to the Turkish border where their papers should allow them immediate access. Hassan said it was advisable to travel through the night and rest under cover during the day. The area outside the environs of Aleppo and en route to the border would be patrolled by both government and rebel forces. They would need to leave the main road and travel cross country, heading toward Afrin, after which it was a further forty miles beyond Midanki to the border.

After a few hours sleep, they spent most of the following day packing the vehicles. Hassan had brought a sub machine gun, two rifles and three pistols. He made a point of giving the young girls a pistol each and gave them a basic education in how to use them. He had also brought along five pairs of night vision glasses. Their mother had baked a selection of meat pasties and cakes and had helped stock the vehicles up with bottles of water.

 Their final meal in the house that had been their family home for over forty years was an emotional affair, particularly for their mother and father. Hamid raised his glass in a toast to the end of the hostilities and hopefully the opportunity for them to return to a normal life in the not too distant future.

They boarded the vehicles shortly after dark and made their way out of the city. They were stopped three times but their papers were accepted without a problem. Guards at one of the checkpoints asked Hassan why he was leaving the city and his unit but he had arranged a week's leave of absence and informed them that he was taking his family to safety and would then return to continue the struggle.

The plan was to head to Afrin through the night, avoiding the main route using mainly single-track roads. They would park up during daylight in one of the vast forests surrounding Afrin and aim to continue their journey after darkness had set in.

They passed many burnt out vehicles en route and there was ample evidence of conflict in some of the small villages they passed through.

Sunlight streamed through the grove in which they had camped and after getting a few hours sleep in their sleeping bags, the girls decided they would go looking for a river to where they could swim after breakfast. Hassan's offer of protection was quickly rejected and the girls set off.

After about ten minutes they found a small river and came across a natural pool shortly afterwards where they were soon splashing around naked and laughing. Selma thought to herself that it was a long time since she had heard laughter in their family.

They were getting ready to leave the pool when they heard the loud crack of a branch. Startled, they turned together to see a young deer looking at them from the bank. It showed no sign of running off as they climbed out of the water but then came the sound of distant gunfire from Afrin and it sped away.

On the way back to their camp, Selma asked her sisters what they hoped to do when they reached Turkey. Yasmin replied that she would like to go to Medical School like Selma and she hoped that her father would be able to pull together some relevant tuition in Turkey.

Sonia was younger and more introverted than her sister. She said that she would help their mother to set up a new home. Selma said that she would work as a doctor in the refugee camps until she made a decision on her medical career.

Yasmin asked her if she had a boyfriend at the hospital. Selma shook her head and said that there was no time for proper relationships and that she was not in favour of casual sex. This set the girls off giggling and making faces at each other. It was good that the incident with the Al Qaeda soldiers had not left them emotionally damaged.

Before they mounted up Hassan said that they needed to travel without headlights after they left the forest. They would weave their way across the open country to the west of Midanki. This would be the most difficult part of their journey not only because of the terrain but because it carried the highest risk of encountering government-backed troops.

Everything went well for the first four hours, although they frequently needed all the traction of the four-by-fours to traverse the rocky plain. They had just completed their descent onto the valley floor when disaster happened.

Out of nowhere a large beam of flight swept the ground ahead of the lead vehicle before locking onto it. A Syrian voice bellowed out from a microphone telling them to stop and get out of their vehicles and wait to be taken prisoner.

Hassan tried desperately to escape the beam, but without success. Hamid shouted at Selma to let him get out and then to drive away in the opposite direction as fast as she could. She was going to refuse and track Hassan when Hamid opened the door and rolled out onto the sand.

Up ahead, the helicopter fired two rockets, which narrowly missed Hassan's vehicle, and two jeeps carrying three armed soldiers each appeared from the gloom some four hundred yards behind the fugitives.

Selma was shell-shocked by the sudden turn of events. All of a sudden she heard the crack of a single rifle shot and one of the soldiers fell out of the right hand jeep. It was her father who was trying to give Hassan a chance of escaping.

The vehicle swung round and headed in the direction the rifle shot had come from firing rapidly from the machine gun that was fixed to the rear canopy. Hamid got off a few more shots but did not stand a chance and was riddled with bullets as he tried to break cover and find a better defensive position.

Up ahead, a blinding flash of light illuminated the darkness. The helicopter's third rocket had hit Hassan's jeep, which burst into flames and rolled over and over, casting out the bodies of its occupants. Selma screamed but could not turn away as events unfolded. There were four bodies lying on the sand, two of which crawled slowly away from the jeep.

Soldiers arrived on the scene while the helicopter circled above, illuminating the carnage below. One of the soldiers got out of his vehicle. He carried a pistol and walked slowly over to each of the bodies in turn. Two bodies were barely moving and Selma cried out in pain as he fired two bullets into them and they became still.

All five of the remaining soldiers approached the final body. It was Hassan. He raised himself into a seated position. Selma could make out his profile as one of the soldiers kicked a knife out of his hand, which then hung limply by his side.

Selma came to her senses and used her professional training to evaluate the situation. She had to decide whether to make a run for it in the jeep or try and hide, using the darkness for cover, before trying to find a village the following day and asking for help. She decided on the latter course of action and took the vehicle's keys and a pistol with her. Then she left the cover of the jeep and hurried into the darkness. She found a small hollow where she covered herself with sand and waited.

A series of agonised screams came from the valley below, then silence. It did not take the helicopter long to find her

277

abandoned jeep. The soldiers arrived shortly afterwards and held a discussion, and then one of their jeeps drove off leaving the second with two soldiers, who set about searching the area.

Selma lay hidden over four hundred yards from her jeep and had made sure not to leave any tracks that could be traced.

The two soldiers split up and began walking in ever widening circles away from the jeep, calling out to each other every two minutes. Selma worked out that if they carried on moving at the same pace, it would take them less than half an hour until they found her.

Fortune smiled upon her when the nearest soldier was only about thirty metres away. He stopped and turned around to urinate. Selma was up and out of her hideout quickly and reached him just as he was turning around again. He went to raise his rifle but she slashed the jagged edge of her knife across his unprotected throat. There was a terrible gurgling noise and he collapsed at her feet.

She turned her attention to her other adversary. He clearly had not seen what had happened and she managed to track carefully around behind him so that she was less than twenty yards from the rear of his position.

The man raised his hands to his mouth to call his colleague but instead, he collapsed slowly onto his face with two bullets lodged in the back of his spine.

Selma checked that the soldier was dead and ran to her vehicle. It started up first time and she drove carefully down into the valley to see if any of her family remained alive.

She stopped beside her father's body, which had bled out into the surrounding sand. He had six bullet wounds in his torso and head. She sat for a minute opposite his body saying an impromptu goodbye, then bent over the corpse and kissed him twice on his forehead. She dragged his beloved body through the sand then hauled him into the back of the jeep, before driving down to the burnt out vehicle on the floor of the valley. Selma needed all of her professional training to cope with the scene that confronted her.

Hassan's body had been mutilated while he was still alive. An eye had been gouged out and several fingers cut off. Finally he had been shot through the forehead. Selma could not stop herself and turned away to be sick at the sight of her handsome brother. She returned and kissed his damaged head.

The two bodies face down in the sand belonged to her sisters. They had been badly injured when the rocket hit the jeep but had tried to crawl away. Both had been shot in the back of the head. Tears were now rolling down Selma's cheeks as she turned them over and kissed them both. It was pointless to check either of them for a pulse.

Her mother's charred remains were inside the vehicle. Selma prayed that the explosion had killed her instantly. In less than five minutes, Selma's whole family had been killed in front of her.

She slumped down in the sand and rested her back against her jeep. She needed to think what to do next. Her first priority was the burial of her family. She could take them to a nearby village and try to arrange for a proper burial or she could dig a hole and bury them here in the desert.

There was no right answer and she fell asleep, exhausted as she considered her awful dilemma. She awoke to see two men standing over her with rifles and ten men examining the area where her parents' bodies lay. One of the men who appeared to be in charge broke off and approached Selma. 'Good morning Madame, my name is Kemal Affaly. I am a captain with the People's Defence Front and these are my men. Can you tell me what happened here last night?'

Selma was relieved by his words, as the PDF were bitter enemies of the Syrian Government. Selma told him her story, beginning from when she and her family left Aleppo.

'You jumped out of the frying pan and into the fire. Please accept my sympathy for your terrible loss. Would you like my men to bury your family here or take them to the nearest village where they can be buried if you leave a donation?'

Selma plumped for the latter option, paid the captain and offered a further sum if the village Imam would say some words during the burial. The captain suggested that they take the bodies to Sindif, a nearby village.

They were on their way in fifteen minutes. The captain rode with Selma in her jeep and gave directions. He asked if she had thought about what she would do. Selma said she would decide in the next few days whether she would carry on to a refugee camp or go back to the hospital in Aleppo.

'Can I suggest a third alternative? Become part of my unit and help us exact revenge for your family. We hunt government patrols and supply convoys and have killed hundreds of the dictator's soldiers. Having a doctor with us would save many lives when my men are injured.'

Selma promised him an answer after her parents' burial and Kemal found a family who said she could stay with them for the next few days. He said that if she opted to cross the border, they would travel with her and see her across but he would have to commandeer her jeep.

The funeral took place the following evening and most of the villagers attended. Death was no stranger to anyone living in Syria. After the Imam said a few words, Kemal's men fired a volley.

Selma felt as if her body was an empty shell. She did not want to go back to the hospital and face friends of her family, so she decided to accept Kemal's offer.

The following day they drove to PDF headquarters in a deserted village, some sixty kilometres from Aleppo. Kemal got Selma to formally enlist and organised a doctor's uniform for her. It was a tight fit and she could see him

looking at her nipples, which protruded against the tight

camouflage material. He blushed profusely as she caught

him watching her.

Awakening

Over the next year, Selma earned the nickname of 'The Black Angel' not only because of the many times she saved the lives of PDF soldiers, but also because of the numerous occasions on which she used her medical knowledge to torture captured government soldiers for information. Her Hippocratic oath had died on that fateful night on the Midanki plain.

Winter came and the PDF squad spent many nights huddled around campfires in caves in the mountains. Selma had become close to Kemal. They had plenty in common as his family had been taken as hostages and shot by government forces in retribution for a PDF attack.

One night shortly before Christmas, there was a screech of tyres at the entrance to the cave and shouts of 'Selma, come quickly!' Three of the squad's jeeps had run into an ambush and were badly shot up.

Four bodies were carried out and Selma's heart skipped a beat when she realized that Kemal was one of them. She quickly examined all four. Two men were dead and the fourth had a through and through wound in his lower leg. Selma shouted for one of the medics to deal with the minor injury and had Kemal carried on a stretcher to her makeshift operating theatre.

Kemal was unconscious, having passed out from the pain caused by the two bullets embedded in his back. It took two hours to remove the bullets, during which time he lost a fair amount of blood. At the end of the operation Selma dressed his wounds and ordered him to be taken to the warmest area of the cave where a fire was lit near his bed.

Two days went by in which Kemal passed in and out of consciousness. He had a raging fever and alternated between shivering violently and sweating profusely. Selma looked after him personally, which was just as well as he regularly called out her name saying that he wanted her and that he loved her.

During the middle of the second night, Selma got up, brought over some screens, put them around Kemal's bed and put out the fire. She undressed completely in the ensuing dark and climbed in bed beside him. For a while Kemal continued to shiver uncontrollably, but gradually calmed as she stroked his forehead. Selma got up before dawn came, dressed and relit the fire.

Later that morning, Kemal began to improve and his fever waned. By the following evening he was able to sit up in bed when Selma brought him some soup. He smiled at her and said 'I thought I was drifting away last night, but then I think I was visited by an angel who pulled me back. A black angel.'

It was Selma's turn to blush, but she did not take her hand away when he reached out and took it. From then on she visited Kemal's bed and lay with him every night. The pair did not need to talk. Instead, Selma lay with her head on his chest and listened to his heartbeat.

Kemal managed to arrange two-week's convalescence leave for both of them and the couple spent fourteen idyllic days on the Syrian resort coastline, during which their relationship blossomed into love. It was Selma's first ever love affair and the thrill of it re-ignited her feelings generally and passion for medicine in particular, as the awful emptiness that had filled her over the last year began to break down.

Not long after they returned to camp, Kemal was promoted to the rank of colonel and was given command of one of the PDF battalions near the front line in Aleppo. Selma immediately applied for a surgeon's post at the hospital where she had previously worked and was quickly appointed.

The next year was one of the happiest in her life. She and Kemal moved into her family home, which had survived the bombings almost intact. Time was at a premium for both of them so they made the most of every precious minute they shared. Selma cultivated a small garden at the back of the house and grew flowers as a reminder of the love and happiness she had enjoyed as a child there.

Holiday seasons were strange for her and Kemal, as they had no surviving family so they tended to arrange a few days together in a hotel on the coast or in the mountains. The war was not going well and rebel territory shrank as Government troops fought their way forward, supported by Russian air strikes. The Americans seemed reluctant to increase their support as ISIS units had begun to fight alongside the rebels.

One day, as Selma was completing her post surgical rounds, her phone vibrated in her coat pocket. She looked at the text message and gasped.

'Goodbye my darling. You were the love of my life. X x x'

She told her assistant to finish the rounds and ran out of the hospital as fast as she could to her car. She could not remember anything of her ten-minute journey to PDF Headquarters. She waved her identity papers as she passed through the layers of security and made her way to her husband's office.

Kemal's superior officer was waiting in the office and rose to meet her. 'Where is Kemal?' she blurted out. 'Is he ok?'

The general put his arm on her shoulder. 'I am so sorry my dear. Kemal's battalion became cut-off after a counter attack and was wiped out by a heavily armed government force, supported by helicopters.'

'He could have been taken prisoner!' said Selma desperately.

'I am afraid not. The government has not been taking any prisoners for the last three months. Kemal was blown up at his command post during a helicopter attack.'

What the general did not say was that Kemal's unit was supposed to be backed up by a large Al Qaeda reserve unit which would have enabled them to retreat under-cover, but the AQ soldiers had broken ranks and left the PDF to their fate.

Once again, life had left Selma alone and abandoned.

Camp Life

The next few months revolved around Selma's work, which kept her focused and stopped her thinking of the black void that filled her mind. Her only other escape was to tend her garden at the house. Following Kemal's death she added a vine tree and arranged for a neighbor to water the garden when she had several day shifts in succession at the hospital.

Selma talked continuously to her flowers and plants, who all had identities. One day she was tilling the soil when a jeep pulled up outside her house and Moussa got out. He'd been Kemal's number two during their days in the mountains. After exchanging greetings she invited him into the house and made tea.

After further pleasantries, Moussa got down to the purpose of his visit. Kemal had spoken of his and Selma's feelings for each other and said that if anything ever happened to him, Moussa had to tell Selma that she should leave Aleppo and all of its memories and follow her career. She should not squander her abilities and waste her love in what was becoming a barren wilderness.

After a while, Moussa's message began to take effect and Selma thought about what she should do. She came round to thinking that she should leave Syria and look for a job elsewhere in the Middle East or in Europe where her excellent English language skills would help her to adapt.

She made an application to Medicine Sans Frontiers, hoping that if she served in the refugee camps or in Africa for the organization, that it would act as a springboard for a permanent job in a hospital.

Three months later, following an extensive interview process, initially via Skype and subsequently at the hospital where she worked, Selma was appointed Senior Medical Officer at the Kilis Öncüpınar Camp in Turkey, adjacent to the Syrian Border.

Selma took up her post at the beginning of 2015. The camp was the first to be constructed after the start of the war and housed some fifteen thousand Syrian Refugees, part of the two point three million existing in Turkey. It was purpose built, consisting of some two thousand containers, which were linked by brick paths. There were seven schools and four kindergartens, plus a large number of shops designed to meet the needs of an itinerant population.

The camp held two types of refugee. Those who were transitory and were using the camp as a stop off en route to

Europe, with a view to earning economic migrant status, and those who wished to return to Syria when it was safe to do so. People in the latter group tended to stay longer in the camp, where most families had undergone loss and suffering.

Medical facilities at Kilis were good and major surgery could be carried out there. MSF saw that adequate supplies of equipment and drugs were maintained.

This was not always the case at the newer camps and part of Selma's role was to visit the other camps in their region and take stock of how the medical units were coping and transfer in resources if needed.

She soon came to terms with the job and set up the equivalent of a general practitioner's clinic to deal with the ongoing illnesses and complaints of the thousands of refugees in the camp. She also established a small hospital, backed up by two operating theatres to deal with more serious injuries such as bullet and shrapnel wounds.

Sex crimes were also prevalent, particularly against teenage girls and Selma carried out a number of abortions in her first year. She set up a family planning clinic for women of all ages, as conceiving a child was not a great idea in such a difficult environment. Through her work Selma came into contact with countless numbers of families whose lives had been destroyed by the conflict, like her own.

Hundreds of families had lost one or both parents and Selma was amazed by the resilience that the survivors showed. Many of them set out on journeys to Europe, which involved travelling hundreds of miles on foot over difficult terrain.

One family in particular made a lasting impression on her. Hassan was fifteen years of age and had been carried into the camp hospital with his right arm badly wounded. His three sisters had significant shrapnel wounds caused by a barrel bomb exploding near their house in Midanki.

Selma operated on the whole family and managed to save Hassan's arm. She removed all of the shrapnel from the bodies of his siblings. The family had a three-week convalescence in one of the camp wards and Selma got to know them well as she chatted to them daily on her rounds.

Hassan was a talented pianist and he planned to study music at university. Their parents had both been teachers but were blown to bits by the aircraft strike.

When they were discharged Selma arranged accommodation for them and made a point of dropping in on them regularly. She was inspired by their determination to make a success of their lives, which Hassan said they owed to their parents' memory.

Hassan's elder sister Marion had taken over the role of 'mother' for the family and she often called in on Selma and asked to discuss major issues that affected their family group.

After a year, during which Hassan and his family all got part time jobs at the camp, the siblings saved up enough money to pay for a boat trip from Greece to the Italian mainland. When spring arrived they set off to walk the seven hundred and fifty miles to the coast.

Selma brought food from the kitchens for the family to help them on their journey and bade them an emotional farewell.

She gave Hassan her mobile number and told him that she would always do what she could to help them.

Inter racial rivalries and the mafia-type structures that proliferated often caused problems in the camps. Drug theft and drug usage was widespread, particularly among the younger refugees whose lives were monotonous and free of motivational structures.

Late one afternoon, Selma was finishing up one of her inspections at a neighbouring camp. She told her colleague and security guard that she was just going to check the level of medical supplies in case more drugs were required to support the medical team.

She walked to the Medical Supplies Tent, which had a small administration area at the front and a locked secure unit at the rear where medical supplies and computers were kept when the post was not manned.

Selma was alarmed to see that the door to the secure area was wide open. There was no sign of the security guard. She raised her mobile phone to her mouth to ring her colleague and get him to raise the alarm when two youths jumped out in front of her. They looked as if they were in their late teens. Both were armed with rifles and they carried large daggers in their hands.

'Put your phone down or we will kill you!' shouted the tallest youth. Selma did as she was told and the youths pushed her inside the secure area where the security guard lay motionless on the floor. The young men had hacked open a large number of drug containers and filled up two mobile containers, ready to make their escape.

The two were in conversation and Selma could she was the talking point. They were deciding whether or not to kill her. Selma decided that she would not risk staying to be stabbed or shot and made a break for it. She thought she had made it to the perimeter when she heard the sound of shots and felt a burning sensation in her left shoulder.

She kept running and glanced over her shoulder. Her attackers had given up the pursuit and were loading their containers into a jeep ready to flee. Selma turned a corner to see her colleagues running toward her before blackness fell upon her.

Selma woke to find herself in a hospital bed in the camp's medical unit. Her wound had been dressed and she was hooked up to a drip. It was dark outside and she was in a small ward in which there were several patients and at the far end of the room, a nurse.

Selma gradually began to clear the fog from her head and beckoned the nurse over. 'Where am I and who operated on me?'

The nurse told her that she had been flown by helicopter to Kilis camp and that a new doctor who had just arrived from MSF had carried out emergency surgery. His name was Patterson. Selma had lost a lot of blood and it was touch and go for a while but the bullet had been removed and her wound stitched. She was hooked up to a drip and was receiving blood transfusions and intravenous antibiotics.

It was not long before Selma drifted back to sleep and when she woke again it was daylight. The nurse approached her bed accompanied by a tall, suntanned, sandy haired Greek god.

'Ms. Mustafa I presume?' spoke the Greek god with a smile that would have melted the North Pole. 'I was due to report to you today for duty, but there is nothing like getting straight into action. You are a very lucky woman, the bullet was lodged pretty close to your heart and it was tricky getting it out. Here it is, a souvenir for your grandchildren.'

He placed the bullet on her bedside table then turned with his hand extended. 'Chris Patterson at your service.'

All Selma could think about was that this man had seen her naked and had touched her breasts! She blushed profusely and instinctively pulled the bed covers up as she extended her hand. He smiled as he took it as if he was reading her mind.

'We need to make sure transfusions occur seamlessly as you lost a lot of blood before I got my hands on you, and we must guard against infection too. I have heard from my colleagues that you are a complete workaholic, but it is vital that you get complete rest if you are to make a swift recovery.'

'It would help if I could go through my diary with you and talk about protocols.' said Selma.

'Let's make that a date for tomorrow at five then.' said Doctor Patterson and smiled at her again as he exited.

The following evening he came to Selma's bedside with two cups of cappuccino and her work diary. The two doctors spent the evening going through Selma's most important tasks and meetings so that he could deputise for her. They also discussed the protocols that Selma had introduced over the last year, and she could not help but be impressed by the manner in which he absorbed them and suggested amendments, most of which were improvements.

He said his goodbye at ten thirty and Selma found that she could not sleep. She rang the head nurse and asked if she would bring her Chris' personnel file the next morning.

She was off the drip now and was able to read Chris's file while having her breakfast.

He was thirty-two years old and had been born in Hastings. He had been a surgical registrar at Brighton General Hospital for five years after qualifying, and had been with MSF for the last three years, working mainly in Africa and the Middle East. She could not help but notice that he had never been married.

That evening he called at the end of his rounds and took her out for some fresh air in a wheelchair, ostensibly to update her on medical events, although he asked a number of personal questions which rarely failed to make her blush. As he escorted her back to her bed he asked if she would like to go on a historical tour in his jeep as part of her convalescence. She smiled and said yes but that it would be a work thing and under no circumstances should he consider it to be a date. The trip would take place on Wednesday, in two day's time.

Wednesday came and Selma found herself taking extra time in the shower and afterwards getting dressed. She had to be careful not to get her wound wet and her shoulder was still really sore. Chris arrived at around half-past-nine and escorted her to his vehicle.

They spent the morning going to two well-known sites of historical interest, two of the hundreds of amphitheatres scattered around Turkey. Then they stopped for a leisurely lunch at a leafy taverna.

They conversed easily and Selma found that she told him most of the important things in her life to date. He said he enjoyed the freedom from bureaucracy in MSF but that he missed his family back in England. She asked him if he missed anyone else and he flashed her that smile and said he had always found that his job worked against forming long-term attachments.

In the afternoon they went for a drive along the beautiful Turkish coastline. Selma did not realise how much the outing had taken out of her and she fell asleep for the latter part of the drive. When she awoke, they were looking out towards the peerless turquoise sea from the top of a deserted promontory.

Chris asked her if she was feeling OK and she nodded, saying 'I didn't realise how little energy I have. I'm sorry for drifting off.'

'Don't worry about not having any energy. It means you wont be able to stop me doing this.'

Chris reached over and kissed Selma gently on the mouth. She did not resist him and felt a feeling of incredible warmth spread through her body.

They sat and talked until it turned dark, stopping to kiss gently several times. Then, reluctantly, they set off back to camp.

Selma returned to work two weeks later. In the interim she and Chris had been out for two meals at local restaurants and another drive into the interior. She was back on her feet properly now and on the last day before her return Chris suggested that they go to the beach for a swim, as the salt water would be good for her wound.

Selma felt a little self-conscious as they lay side by side on the beach. She had an ugly scar at the top of her back but Chris seemed not to notice and spent a lot of time nuzzling her neck and stroking her thighs. She broke away and said 'OK. Time for a swim!'

She ran into the water on the deserted beach. 'I'm coming!' said Chris, as he sprang to his feet and ran towards the water behind her.

As Chris got to the edge of the sea, Selma turned towards him, smiled and said 'it just occurred to me that you have seen me completely naked and I have not had the pleasure.'

'We can soon cure that.' he said dropping his trunks and moving towards her, naked.

Selma reciprocated and they were quickly entwined in the surf. She could feel his erection pressing against her as they held each other close and kissed for what seemed an eternity.

Then Chris led her back to the beach and lay down with her. His lips explored her breasts and then moved downward. Selma moaned and said 'Take me now Chris. Now.'

He climbed on top of her and placed some towels under her shoulder before spreading her legs wide apart and thrusting into her. She held him closer and closer, feeling her juices flow as he slowly moved in and out of her before building up to a climax.

Selma gasped as he erupted inside her. Afterwards they lay side by side for half an hour, feeling the sun caress their naked bodies. She told him that she was not using any contraception and he said that it did not matter to him but she could get a morning after pill if she wished.

That prompted her to climb on top of him for a long slow coupling which ended with them both coming at the same time. They got dressed and he drove them to their favourite restaurant for dinner. Afterward they spent the night together in her rented apartment.

Selma faced a lot of knowing looks from her female colleagues when she returned to work. Everyone told her that she was positively glowing and said she was an advert for Chris's medical skills.

The couple soon settled into a rhythm at work and after a month they moved in together. Selma felt really nervous when she found out that she was pregnant, but Chris was delighted. The following night, he got down on one knee at their usual place for dinner and asked her to become his wife. She was taken aback and had never thought about getting married. Staying together yes, but getting married?

'What will your family think about you marrying a Muslim?' she said.

'There is only one way to find out.' Said Chris. 'I have booked us a week's leave and two flights back to the UK. My mum is really looking forward to meeting you.'

Motherhood and A Return To Family Life

Chris's family house turned out to be a small country estate. Butterflied fluttered in Selma's stomach as the airport taxi wound its way up the drive to where four people stood waiting on the steps.

Chris's mum, Heather, ran towards them as they unloaded their luggage. She hugged Chris first and then turned towards Selma with her arms outstretched. 'Welcome to our home my darling. I hope that it will always feel like your home too.'

Selma could feel genuine warmth emanating from Heather who was clearly delighted that her son was truly happy.

The older man stepped forward and hugged Chris. 'Good to have you back home son.'

He turned to Selma and kissed het lightly on both cheeks. 'Welcome Selma, I look forward to getting to know you.'

Finally, Chris's younger brother Stephen and his sister Melanie came forward and welcomed the newly returned couple.

That evening, the now enlarged family enjoyed an excellent four-course meal cooked by Heather. Both Chris and Selma did not take alcohol with the dinner, which brought sarcastic comments from Stephen, aimed at Chris.

Heather asked Selma if they were hoping for a boy or a girl. She did not sit on the fence. 'I hope we have a boy so that we can restart my family line.'

Thomas, Chris's father, said 'Chris told us about the trauma you endured during your escape from Aleppo. We are so sorry for what you had to endure.'

Selma replied 'I thought my life was over, but Allah has a plan for everyone. Meeting Chris has given me a purpose and brought me a love that I thought I would never discover.'

Melanie asked quite sharply 'What religion are you going to bring your child up in?'

Chris replied for both of them. 'We will allow our children to make a choice of religion when they are old enough to know their own minds. Until then we will teach them the fundamentals of both the Muslim and Christian religions.'

The following morning Stephen took Chris into town to meet some of his friends and Heather took Selma for a walk around their estate, stopping to pick some fresh flowers on the way. 'It is so peaceful here.' Selma said. 'I can understand that it must be a haven for Christopher away from the perpetual conflict and misery that we are faced with on a daily basis.'

Heather replied. 'We have not seen much of Chris over the last three years since he left to join MSF. I hope that will change now that he is going to be a father. Have you talked about where you are going to live after the baby is born?'

'We never seem to stop discussing it. There would be obvious advantages in coming to the UK in that we would both be able to continue our careers, as childcare is affordable and easy to access. We plan on coming back twice more before the baby is born so that I can make up my mind about whether I would like to live in Britain. My family's assets have now been transferred to me and we would be able to buy a house.'

'That's great news Selma. Let me know if there is anything I can do to help. Chris's father and I would be more than willing to help out with childcare arrangements. Oh, and I thought I would take you shopping in London with me before you return to Turkey and you can pick out some baby things.'

Selma said that she would like that very much and that she would like to make the family a traditional Syrian meal before she left, as a means of saying thank you.

On their way back to the house, Heather said 'You will probably have noticed that Melanie has been more reserved toward you than the rest of the family. I think I should tell you the reason for this. Chris was the childhood sweetheart of Melanie's best friend Hannah. They moved in together when he qualified as a doctor and were planning on getting married when Hannah was killed in a car crash. Chris was devastated and rootless and a year later he left the hospital to join MSF. Melanie has never recovered from losing her best friend, and I think she is jealous that Chris has found meaning in his life again.'

Selma was taken aback by this revelation but thanked Heather for telling her. That evening when they were lying in bed she told Chris what his mother had said.

'I am sorry my darling. I should have told you before we returned to England but it took me a long time to finish the grieving process and I did not want to reopen my feelings. I love you as much as it is possible for a man to love a woman and I hope you know that I plan to spend the rest of my life proving that to you.'

Selma leaned over him, took off her nightgown and they spent the rest of the night putting the ghosts of their past behind them.

Selma's trip to London with Chris's mum and sister was a great success. The shopping was divided between planning for a nursery and buying essential items for the forthcoming birth, and shopping for clothes where Selma allowed herself to be 'managed' by Melanie.

In no time at all it was time for them to fly back to Turkey, but not before Selma had cooked a traditional Syrian buffet. Some of Heather and Thomas's friends and Stephen and Melanie attended and the evening was a huge success, especially after the impromptu cabaret provided by Melanie and Selma, who performed a belly dancing routine in full costume.

Chris insisted that Selma performed a private routine when they retired and it was noticeable how tired they both were at breakfast the following morning.

Once back in Turkey the lovers decided that their future lay in England. Both gave three months notice to MSF as it would be quite a blow for them to leave the camp together, so much so that in the end Chris worked on a further month.

They decided that they would get married when they next returned to England would look to buy a house before the baby was born. Chris would apply for Medical Registrar's jobs on the south coast and the plan was for Selma to apply for Surgical or Medical registrars jobs six months after the birth.

Things went pretty much to plan. Chris was offered a registrar's post at Chichester Hospital while he and Selma were house-hunting in the area, so they concentrated their efforts on that city and ended up buying a three bedroomed town house.

The wedding was a quiet family affair. Heather insisted that it was held at the estate and that she would do the catering. Selma invited two of her work colleagues to be her bridesmaids. Melanie was definitely not impressed when Selma was happy to have the 'obey' promise included in the bridal undertakings.

Less than three months later and Selma was on her way in Chris's car to the maternity ward. She felt happy beyond belief as she knew that her child would be safe and be part of a large and caring family.

PART 5

Marion's Story

Orphaned

Marion pushed through the throng of children standing in front of the school notice board where that year's exam results were posted as usual. It was a time for celebration in many homes, though there were extra chores for those who had not performed well. Marion had not yet reached the Board when her two friends, Miriam and Jasmin, came running up and hugged her.

'You have done it again!' said Miriam. 'Top of year. You will be certain to get admitted to university after next year's exams and we both got good marks too. Lets meet for a celebratory milk shake at McDonald's later.'

Sure enough, Marion saw that she was first in class and she walked on to the school office to get a copy of her annual report to take home to her parents. They were already extremely proud of her and she was determined to make them even prouder by going to university and becoming a doctor.

Her father owned the Baker's shop in the east of Midanki and her mother helped out with the business, as well as running a home with four children. That night the family had a celebratory meal and the children were each given a piece of a special cake that their father had baked in Marion's honour.

Marion was allowed to meet her friends later but had to be back home by ten thirty. As usual there were two topics of conversation, their plans for the future, and boys. Jasmin had a boyfriend at school, who walked her home each evening and she kept the girls informed of his unsuccessful attempts to get his hands up her skirt and inside her blouse.

'Allah loves a trier.' said Miriam, who secretly wished that she had a boyfriend. If that ever happened the lad in question would be a lot more successful at exploring what lay beneath her blouse than Jasmin's beau.

The following afternoon after school the friends were playing a game of 'The Farmers Wife' in the field behind Marion's father's bakery with some younger children from the village. Laughter rang out as several of the players tried to cheat when the Farmer's back was turned.

Suddenly there was a massive explosion and the bakery became a smoking ruin. Several of the children playing the game were blown to pieces. Most of the rest were injured to some extent and a huge pall of smoke hung above the field.

Marion checked herself over. She was covered in cuts and slumped to the ground in a daze. Miriam was in a similar condition ten metres away but Jasmin lay in a pool of dark blood, twenty metres away. Her legs had been blown off.

The sound of ambulance sirens broke the stillness that had descended and a rescue operation began, but there was no rescue for the inhabitants of the bakery, which had taken a direct hit from two barrel bombs, dropped at long range by a Syrian army jet. It was a smoking ruin and there were body parts strewn around the entire area.

After the blast Marion's brother, Hassan, wandered around in a daze. He had been in the bakery and was just leaving with some loaves for home when the bomb hit. He was covered in blood down his right side and his right arm, with which he had been carrying the bread, hung limply by his side.

Two doctors soon arrived at the scene and began to assess the wounded. They decided to send some ambulances to the hospital in Midanki and some to the nearby refugee camp at Kilis Öncüpınar, which had excellent medical facilities.

Marion had multiple shrapnel wounds and needed a blood transfusion, while Hassan was in urgent need of an operation to try to save his arm. It was decided that they would be sent to Kilis. Marion managed to tell the nurse to contact her uncle and get him to make sure that he and his wife took in her two younger sisters Mina who was twelve and Fatima who was ten years of age.

She lost consciousness on the high-speed journey to Kilis and woke up early the following morning. She was lying in bed in a hospital ward and was heavily bandaged. A nurse came to the bed and asked how she was and she replied that she felt woozy. 'That will be the effect of the morphine. Some of your cuts were quite deep and you needed something for the pain after we sanitized them '

'How is my brother Hassan?' asked Marion.

'He is in the next ward' said the nurse. 'He is still unconscious following his operation. Your uncle and his wife and your two sisters are in the waiting room and I will get a message to them telling them you are OK. They can come back at visiting time this afternoon.'

Marion drifted back off to sleep and when she awoke again, the loss of her parents began to hit her, and she sobbed uncontrollably. The whole core of her life and that of her siblings had been removed.

Later that morning a woman doctor came to her bedside and introduced herself as Doctor Mustafa. She checked Marion's dressings and explained that the surgical team had extracted a good deal of shrapnel from various parts of her body. The main risk was infection so she would be closely monitored until her cuts had healed.

Marion asked about Hassan and Doctor Mustafa told her that they had operated for several hours and saved his arm, though if his wounds became septic this could lead to amputation. Hassan was still sedated but should be able to see visitors tomorrow.

At visiting time Marion's uncle Joshua, his wife and Marion's sisters came to her bedside. She could see her sisters had been crying. Everyone came up to her and kissed her on the forehead. Her aunt told her not to worry and said that she would look after her nieces until Marion and Hassan were better, and then they could have a family conference.

Her uncle said that they would delay the funeral ceremony for her parents until Marion and Hassan could attend. This triggered off a fresh bout of sobbing.

Hassan came round the next day and family meetings were held at his bedside, as he was nominally the head of the family now. The funeral was held the following week and Marion and Hassan attended in wheelchairs. After the ceremony, their uncle asked the two eldest children to sit in his parlour. He told the siblings that he had been to see their father's bank manager.

Their parents had some savings and Joshua suggested that they authorise the transfer of these funds to him. He promised to use them to fund their upbringing over the next few years.

Over the next two weeks Marion talked for hours with Hassan about their future. If they stayed I Midanki it was not certain that they would be able to go to university. That was their shared ambition but if they stayed there would be pressure on them to start work and bring in money. The alternative would be for the children to live together for a while in the camp before using their parents' money to try to make it to Europe where they could start a new life. Marion said that she would delay her ambitions to go to university and look after their sisters until they had finished at school.

They asked Doctor Mustafa for advice and after they had spoken three times they decided to live in the camp for a while and then set off for Europe. Doctor Mustafa arranged accommodation for them as well as paid part time work for

Hassan in the camp supermarket, and Marion in medical administration.

Joshua and his wife were not pleased with the decision as it turned out that their parents' savings amounted to almost ten thousand pounds. In their minds a considerable element of it had already been spent.

Over the next year the siblings became a tight family unit and every Friday night all four children sat and planned their journey to Europe. Doctor Mustafa often attended and brought pizzas. She said that she would write them letters when they were ready to go which might make up for their lack of official Turkish papers.

Hassan and Marion gradually recovered from their injuries and Hassan began to play the piano again. It was his ambition to become a concert pianist. Doctor Mustafa arranged for him to give a recital and the donations she collected went into their travel fund.

Marion grew into womanhood and often saw some of the men looking at her figure. One day she was doing some shopping in the camp supermarket when a man came up to her. He introduced himself as Soli and said that he ran the camp nightclub. He told her that she was really beautiful and that he could offer her a job as a hostess. If she accepted, she would be well paid and could earn extra money by being nice to his customers. Marion blushed, as he looked her up and down with a leering grin. She said that she was not interested and hurried off to the tills. She heard him say 'I can wait, especially for a body like yours.

If At First You Don't Succeed

Her encounter with Soli made Marion determined that she and her should leave the camp as soon as possible, and in four weeks they were set to depart. They all had sturdy rucksacks and sleeping bags and enough water, dried meat and chocolate to act as emergency food. Doctor Mustafa gave Hassan a letter, as promised, and she had tears in her eyes as she stood at the gate and waved them goodbye.

With Doctor Mustafa's help, the plan they had decided upon was to head to Gaziantep a main population centre in the south of Turkey. From there they would get a bus to Mersin, then on to the city of Antalya, from where they would try to go by rail to Istanbul. From Istanbul they would catch the Bosporus Ferry to Athens and then make their way to

Patras, which was the main departure point for refugees seeking to cross the Mediterranean to Italy.

Doctor Mustafa had arranged a lift to take them to the main road into Gaziantep, some sixty kilometres away from the camp. Once they reached the road and said goodbye to the driver, the children set off to walk the one hundred kilometres or so into the town.

It was extremely hot but there was no complaining from the young children as they had all discussed what they would have to go through.

There were groups of other refugees on the road and they all offered each other encouragement. They were fortunate to get a lift in a farmer's truck, which saved them thirty kilometres on foot, but still had to spend three nights in villages along the route. They managed to negotiate accommodation and food in two of the villages but had to spend one night out under the stars. It turned extremely cold but they were protected by their sleeping bags.

They arrived in Gaziantep on the fourth day and after a proper meal were able to locate the bus station and bought single tickets to go to Mersin. The journey would take around five hours. Turkey is a vast country and when they got to Mersin they would still have almost one thousand kilometres to travel before they reached Istanbul.

On their arrival in Mersin they were pleased to find that they were able to afford an overnight stay in a small hotel. It seemed to Marion that the owner asked a lot of questions but she thought perhaps this was normal and went to sleep.

The next morning they travelled to the bus station and were about to buy tickets to go to Antalya when three policemen entered the ticket office.

'Let me see your papers!' said the senior policeman.

Hassan produced Doctor Mustafa's letter. 'This does not give you a legal authority to travel through Turkey. You need to accompany us to the police station.'

The children exchanged worried glances but there was little else they could do. They were searched on arrival and had all of their belongings and assets taken by the policeman on duty.

After an anxious wait of several hours they were taken before the local police commandant who was accompanied by two officials, who said that they were from the Immigration Department.

Marion and her family were told that they were illegal immigrants to Turkey and had no right to travel through the country without official permits. They were to be returned to the camp from which they had travelled and their money would be confiscated to pay for the cost of returning them, though they would be allowed to keep their haversacks and sleeping bags.

The children were devastated at what appeared to be a well-organised scam but there was nothing they could do and the following day they were herded onto an army truck and driven back to Kilis, where Doctor Mustafa was waiting to meet them as they were shown into the camp reception. After they had been processed, she took them for a meal. They were completely dejected but she counseled them to regroup over the next few months as she had got them their old jobs back.

Over the next month they restarted their weekly family meetings. Hassan said that they had a big decision to make. They could go back to Syria and try to build a life in Midanki, although the conflict appeared to have worsened over the last year. Or they could save up and try to make it to Europe again. This time they would have to travel on foot, cross-country, which would be exhausting and which meant it would take almost six months to reach Istanbul.

Despite their heartbreaking set back the children wanted to try again. Doctor Mustafa said that this time she would wire most of their money to Istanbul so that they would not be ripped off again.

At their next family conference Hassan said that it would take them two years of saving in the camp to amass the funds they needed to complete their next journey and pay for the boat trip to Europe, but Marion had other ideas.

She went to see Doctor Mustafa and told her that she had decided to become a hostess and wanted to start practicing birth control. The doctor tried to talk her out of it but soon realized how determined Marion was. 'I do not intend to get married in the next six years. I want to get my degree as soon as we arrive in Europe.' said the young girl.

Marion's next step was to pay a visit to Soli. She bought a sexy dress and spent a long time on her make up that night. She made sure that no one saw her when she slipped out of the hut. When she arrived at the nightclub she asked for Soli in person.

'Well, well, well.' he said as she was shown into his office. 'What can I do for you?'

Marion told him that she was prepared to work as a hostess. She said she was a virgin and was prepared to lose her virginity for the right offer.

Soli thought for a minute then went to lock the door to his office. 'Take your clothes off and if I like what I see I will pay you five hundred dollars myself.'

'I am worth more than that.' said Marion. 'Make it one thousand dollars.'

'For that much you will have to obey me and perform whatever sex acts I want you to.' said Soli.

Marion could see that he was getting excited. She started to take off her dress and her underwear. When she was finished he put one thousand dollars on his desk.

'Let's have a drink first to loosen you up.' he said, opening a bottle of champagne and pouring her a glass.

Marion did not realise that he had slipped some Rohypnol into her drink. Soli beckoned her over to his desk and got her to stand in front of him. He stroked the bottom of her back and made appreciative noises, then slowly slid two fingers into her vagina.

Marion gasped as he began to massage her clitoris and bit down hard on her nipples. She could not remember anything else but woke up several hours later with her head hanging off the side of the bed.

She felt woozy and it took her a while to focus. She ached all over and saw that she had bite marks all over her breasts and on the inside of her upper thighs. She was on her own and noticed that there was a handwritten note lying on the desk beside the thousand pounds and a camera.

The note invited her to rewind the shots on the camera and said that Soli would pay her another thousand pounds for every time she took part in a threesome or orgy. She rewound the camera with some trepidation.

At the beginning of the film, she was giving Soli oral sex and then he positioned her in seven different ways while riding her hard. The soundcard picked up her moans and pleas for him to stop.

However, when he did stop he picked up the telephone and spoke briefly. After five minutes two big men entered the room. They began to caress her nipples and lick her vagina while gradually forcing her legs open. They carried on where Soli had left off performing two on one sex acts for the next hour after which time they got dressed and left leaving Marion face down on the bed.

Marion felt totally ashamed and unclean and went to the bathroom. After standing in a hot shower for thirty minutes, her brain began to function again. What was done was done. No one had forced her to do what she had done. She knew she could never tell anyone about what had happened, especially Doctor Mustafa, as she could not face the medic knowing how she had debased herself.

She needed to earn a further nine thousand pounds or what she had done was meaningless. She was surprised how easy it was to return to her job and act as if everything was normal.

After a few days she went back to see Soli at his office. He told her that she was in demand. He had shown the film to several well-connected men in Turkey and they wanted her and were prepared to pay a lot of money for the privilege. He said that he would teach her a belly dance and pole dancing routine, which she could use as a cabaret before the main event.

Two weeks later Soli contacted her and told her to come to the club that night. She was introduced to two well-dressed Turkish men in their mid forties. They had a hard look in their eyes.

After three drinks they led her to Soli's office. Soli had asked her if she wanted to be drugged again or if she would like to snort some cocaine. She declined. After thirty minutes in which she had been repeatedly sodomised and beaten she regretted her decision and made her mind up to ask Soli for something that would numb her sensations next time.

Two months later she sat in Soli's office and told him that her next party would be her last. To her surprise he said that he welcomed that. He said that he had total respect for her and had grown something approaching a paternal affection for her given her response to the hand that life had dealt her.

More importantly he had something to give her and handed her a brown paper bag. She looked inside and gasped, there was a large amount of money, some five thousand dollars as it turned out, and more importantly, a set of official Turkish papers for herself and her family.

She got up and ran to him and hugged him as he said there was no need for her to take part in any more parties. She could swear that there were tears in his eyes.

Two days later Marion and her family started off on the road again, except for Hassan who had agreed to play a concert performance arranged by Soli for which he was being paid three thousand dollars. Hassan asked Marion how she had come up with the money but she refused to tell him and said that she had not stolen it. Doctor Mustafa knew in her heart of hearts what had happened, but she was the last person to judge anyone in this new world.

They followed the same route as on their first journey, but bypassed Mersin, just to be sure. They were asked to produce their papers when they caught the train from Antalya to Istanbul but these proved to be in order and the family arrived in Istanbul, one week after their departure from Kilis.

They had decided in a family discussion that they would spend a few days exploring Istanbul, using some of the money that Soli had given Marion they checked into a tourist hotel.

Marion and her siblings were awed by the wonderful museums and the sheer grandeur of Istanbul and it was with some reluctance that they left to catch the ferry for Athens.

After a few days of similar sightseeing in Athens, which had its own store of wonders, Marion booked four tickets on the train to go to Patras, which was the main refugee departure point for Europe.

Consigned To The Deep

They could see from the train that the roads to Patras were overflowing with refugees who trudged the final miles of what had been long and exhausting journeys. No doubt many of the families they passed had sustained fatalities on the way and in some cases newborn babies had been brought into the world along the roadside.

When she was in Athens Marion had contacted Doctor Mustafa and the doctor wired her the rest of their money, along with her good luck wishes for their future.

Marion and her siblings soon found out that it was impossible to find accommodation in Patras and the surrounding villages, so they resorted to sleeping outside and trying to wash in the overcrowded refugee facilities the following day.

Marion found out that there were a couple of well-known 'agencies' that could arrange boat travel to Italy and they queued for several hours to get an interview.

It turned out that eastern Europeans who did not inspire a lot of confidence ran the agencies. Marion and her family spent several days at the harbour where they watched the boats leaving for Italy.

'Boat' was a broad description for some of the conveyances they saw leaving the quayside. All were grossly overcrowded and every day the authorities broadcast warnings on a loudspeaker system and reported that thousands of people had perished on the unlawful journey to Italy and that anyone who attempted the trip ran the risk of being sent back. It made no difference. Hundreds left the harbour every day.

Eventually Marion got to speak to one of the agents. He told her that they had to pay a deposit of one thousand euros per person and that they could collect their tickets two days before their journey began. Marion asked about what type of boat they would sail on but was told that they would have to take what they were given. They would all be given a life belt and their journey would take place in one week's time.

The next day Marion queued for bread at one of the bakeries, which brought back memories of her father's bakery. She wondered if her mother and father were watching their family from heaven as they struggled to make a new life for themselves. 'Have you got a date for your departure yet?' came a voice from behind her.

Marion turned to see a handsome young man dressed in shorts, a Ralph Lauren polo shirt and with Skechers on his feet. He smiled at her revealing perfect teeth and she could not resist smiling back as she said 'We leave next Thursday morning.'

'Me too. Perhaps you will let me take you for a cup of coffee when we have collected our bread? My name is Mehmet.'

Marion thought, why not? She had lots of time on her hands and it would be nice to have a conversation with someone other than her brothers and sisters. It did no harm that he was extremely good looking.

Mehmet brought two cappuccinos over to a table and he and Marion spent the next hour finding out about each other. His family home in Aleppo had been destroyed and he was travelling with his younger brother and his parents. His father had worked in a bank and he and his wife had found the trek hard going, but they were confident that things would be better in Europe. Mehmet had a brother who worked in a bank in Germany.

Marion told him her story, leaving out the part about their return visit to the camp. They got on well together and agreed to meet up the following day and go for a walk along the beach.

The beach walk became a daily thing over the next few days and on the day before their departure they exchanged mobile numbers and agreed to meet up in Berlin in three months time. They kissed before parting.

One kiss turned into several and Marion felt a warm feeling envelop her as she and Mehmet waved goodbye. Unbeknown to her, Mina and Fatima had been spying on her and when she got back they re-enacted the kissing scene saying 'Oh Mehmet. Oh Mehmet.'

Marion chased after them, laughing, but could not catch the young rascals.

They collected their haversacks and bedding and set off for the Agency Office first thing on Thursday morning. They were excited and nervous, and the latter feeling increased when they arrived at their boat for their departure. It was a largish flat-bottomed vessel, which was already full to capacity when they arrived, but two of the crew helped them to sit down. They were told to give up their sleeping bags but could keep their haversacks if they put them on. Marion saw Mehmet sitting with his parents and they exchanged waves.

It was anticipated that the crossing would take thirty hours so it was likely to be something of an ordeal, especially as they were crammed onto the boat like sardines. Many of the children onboard were crying when the boat set off.

They had been promised life belts but none were handed out and only members of the crew were equipped with them. They kept shouting out that belts would not be required as the crossing would be quick and safe.

The sea was certainly calm when they set off from Patras under a scorching hot sun. They had thought to wear hats, which were a definite help, as was the water doled out regularly by the crew.

After three hours, the sight of land was behind them and the main challenge was to remain comfortable. The four children passed the time by discussing their futures. They knew they would have to spend some time in a camp in Italy but hoped that the letters Doctor Mustafa had written would help them, along with the fact that they had Turkish papers.

After a further two hours, the wind started to get up. More worryingly, there were several black clouds on the horizon. Panic began to set in when the crew started to pass out tins and told the men to start baling.

The baling seemed to work for a while and they continued to make steady progress. Then the black clouds hit and there was torrential rain and wind. Water started to flood onto the deck and the rear of the boat began to sink slowly.

By now most of the passengers were screaming and there was a massive crush to try to get to the front of the boat, which was being fiercely defended by those in situ. All of a sudden the boat started to sink more quickly. The crew abandoned ship but the male passengers attacked several of them and ripped off their lifebelts. The Captain shouted out that he had sent out an SOS and coastguard vessels would soon be on their way.

Mehmet shouted to Marion that they should jump overboard but hang onto their haversacks. The water looked so blue and inviting but it was freezing and the children were shivering as they swam together holding their haversacks in front of them. Mehmet left his parents and swam over to Marion.

All around them passengers were drowning and there was nothing that they could do to help. They held hands and Marion told them to sing to keep awake as they drifted away from the remnants of the boat and the many people that were clinging to the wreckage.

After thirty minutes the younger children were unconscious while Marion and Mehmet desperately tried to keep them afloat. There was still no sign of a rescue vessel and Marion realized that there was no hope. To think that after all they had been through, it would end here.

Marion leaned over and kissed Mehmet who was shivering violently. She mouthed 'Goodbye' and let go of his hand.

The following day there were media broadcasts about the 'Maria' what had sunk off the coast of Italy. Over one hundred refugees had perished. It did not even rank as a main news item.

PART 6

UNION

Settling Down

Chris paced around the guest room awaiting news of the birth. Selma had had a difficult time and ended up having a Caesarean.

There was another chap sitting in the room. 'This is really stressful isn't it?' he said, smiling at Chris. 'What do you say to a cigarette outside? I would have said a cigar but that's a bit premature.'

Chris replied that he did not smoke but was happy to pop outside for some fresh air. It turned out that Stewart's wife Sofia had been in labour for twelve hours and he was not as calm as his outward demeanor showed.

The call came for Stewart first and he did not need to be asked twice. He was at Sofia's bedside in a trice, just in time to see the birth of a healthy baby boy who came into the world weighing seven pounds and twelve ounces. 'Well done darling. He is beautiful, it is just as well he takes after his mother.'

Sofia lay back on her pillow, her hair soaked in sweat, but Stewart thought to himself that he had never seen her look so beautiful. The midwife passed his son to him and he found it difficult to keep his emotions in check. He had an overwhelming feeling of completeness.

Two doors down the same scene was enacted with the outcome a petite baby girl for Selma and Chris, weighing in at six stone and ten ounces. Selma was pretty tired and Chris said a tender goodnight after he had held his baby daughter. Earlier he had seen tears rolling down Selma's cheeks and when he asked her what was the matter, she had replied 'I so wanted to give you a son.'

He replied with a smile. 'I could not be happier my darling, than with the beautiful daughter you have given me. We will just have to keep trying for a boy!'

The two men bumped into each other on the way to the exit and congratulated each other. Stewart said 'How about going to wet the baby's head?'

'I need to ring my parents first.' said Chris 'But I will meet you in the Horse and Farrier in fifteen minutes.'

The two new fathers got on like a house on fire. Stewart was fascinated by Chris's experiences with MSF, as he had served in the Middle East when he was in the army, and Chris was intrigued by Stewart's sports investment career. They ended up talking football and discovered that they both were Brighton and Hove Albion supporters.

The following day the midwives were keen to get the two new mothers on their feet, even though they were both stiff and sore. They were both exhausted after a visit to the bathroom for a wash, but obeyed the midwives instructions to go and sit in the visitors room for a while and then return and feed their babies. Both women had opted to breast feed and managed their first feeds without too much discomfort.

Sofia asked Selma if she had known the sex of her baby before the birth and she replied saying that she had not. She had been disappointed at first that she had not produced a male child but all of that disappeared when she held her daughter.

Sofia said 'I am so grateful to have given birth to a healthy child. I had to come in early as I had a few complications. The staff are all so wonderful.'

There were two other women in the room who were both in wheelchairs, and one of them had a baby in her arms. She asked 'Is it alright if we come and see your babies when you return to the ward?'

Selma and Sofia said yes and the four women ended up having a cup of tea together. 'My name is Polly.' said the woman with the baby. 'I am recovering from an operation on my back which was carried out two months before the birth. To be honest I am going stir crazy.'

The fourth woman was black and looked like an older teenager. She smiled and said 'My name is Beki and I am pleased to meet you both. I am recovering from a double fracture to my right leg.'

Selma turned to see Sofia looking at Beki with her mouth open. 'Are you Beki the world champion distance runner?'

Beki nodded with a broad smile on her face. 'Yes, but I could not beat either of you in a race to the loo at the moment.'

Everyone laughed and Sofia said 'My husband is a keen sports fan. Would you mind awfully giving him your autograph when he comes to visit me tonight?'

'Of course.' said Beki.

Their daily meetings over a cuppa became a ritual, as did Stewart and Chris's nightcap at the Horse and Farrier. On the third night of their stay, Stewart brought a guest with him. Jamie Mullen was a top young jockey and had ridden one of Stewart's horses that day at Goodwood. Stewart insisted that he should stay overnight as he was riding again the next day. He took Jamie with him to meet Beki in the visitor's room before he went to see Sofia and John, which was the name the parents had decided on, as it was popular in both Polish and English.

Jamie was a cheeky Liverpudlian who introduced himself and said he was awed to be in the presence of a woman who he could not catch, even when he had a horse underneath him.

Beki laughed and Stewart said that he would leave Jamie to entertain her while he went to see his wife and son. He returned later to see the two young people creased with laughter and demonstrating extremely positive body language toward each other. Jamie told Beki he would be back to pick her up the following evening to take her out for a drink on his way home from the races. He had obtained the ward sister's permission to do so.

On their way back to Stewart's house Stewart said 'You cheeky young devil, you never miss a trick.'

Jamie replied saying 'If there is such a thing as love at first sight I have caught it.'

The following evening was going to be the girls' last night in hospital. Stewart rang Sofia and asked her if she would ask the sister if he and Stewart could take them out with Polly and Beki to dinner. The Sister agreed.

When the evening came the girls were waiting outside with Polly in her wheelchair, but there was no sign of Beki.

Apparently she was waiting for Jamie who was driving down from Ascot to take her out.

The newly found friends had a sumptuous meal at one of Stewart's favourite restaurants. The talk drifted round to horses and Polly told them of her background and the death of Spartan. Everyone sympathised but Stewart said 'Tell me where the bastard lives.'

'He ended up paying the penalty.' said Polly, without going into too much detail.

The night ended with them promising to stay in touch and then Chris invited everyone to Sunday lunch at his mum's the following week.

He and Selma decided to call their daughter Hannah, after Selma's mother. Everyone had a marvellous time and it wasn't a great surprise when Jamie and Beki arrived and announced that they were an item.

It did not take long for the media to pick up that they were together and a media circus developed for a week. They had agreed Beki would leave the hospital and live at Jamie's where she would arrange for daily physiotherapy.

Beki faced a nine-month trail back to full fitness and this gave the young lovers a chance to explore their feelings. Beki was now almost twenty and the Olympic Games were coming up in two years. She would not be fit enough for the world championships this year. Her body had changed and she was now a beautiful young woman. However she was almost seven kilograms heavier than when she was breaking world records.

She sat down with Jamie one night and said that it had always been her dream to win an Olympic Gold medal, which would mean training at altitude for six months in both of the next two years. She understood if he could not commit to living without her for that period of time.

Jamie told her that he had been thinking a lot about this and that the last months had been the happiest of his life. He had never been able to commit before but, if Beki felt the same way, he planned on spending the rest of his life with her. She answered by throwing her arms around him and telling him that breaking her leg was the best thing ever to happen to her.

'You had better be damned good at phone sex!' he quipped.

'Never mind that. We will have to cram six month's rations into the next month before I go!'

Beki rang Taresh and told her of her decision and they discussed a training regime leading up to the Olympics. They would start in Addis Ababa in two month's time.

Beki spent the next two months accompanying Jamie to the races and she came to admire both his skills with horses and the bravery he possessed. He regularly rode horses travelling at speeds of over forty miles an hour, with nowhere to go if a horse fell in front of him.

They also had dinner regularly on Sundays with Sofia and Stewart, Polly and Selma and Chris. They all wished her well on her training schedule and said they would keep a close eye on Jamie!

The day came when Beki had to catch her flight to Addis Ababa. They made love all through the previous night and she had never felt so complete. She got up to take a shower and get dressed and stood naked in front of the mirror when Chris, who was lying on the be, said 'I feel so good when I look at that gorgeous butt of yours. Millions of men are going to be watching it every time you race, wishing they were in this position!'

She shrieked with laughter and threw herself on top of him. It was touch and go whether she would be ready for the taxi when it arrived.

Two Years On

Taresh's face broke into a wide smile when she met Beki at airport arrivals in Addis Ababa, her protégé had become a woman in the eighteen months they had been apart and she positively glowed with happiness.

They were soon both surrounded by Beki's family, Bela and a media scrum, who all wanted to know whether she was going to win gold at the Cape Town Olympics as well as details of her romance in England.

Beki was tired after her flight and her long farewell to Jamie and was glad to get back to her house in Addis Ababa. She agreed to have breakfast at Taresh's house with Bela who was one of the favourites for the long jump gold.

At breakfast she never stopped laughing when Bela plied her with questions about Jamie and their sex life. Bela's little girl ran around happily and played while the women talked. She left with Taresh to go to the National Athletics Centre and start planning her Olympics campaign.

Taresh told her what she already knew. She would have to train harder than she had ever done to reduce her body weight and get the bank of miles built up in her legs. A serious rival had emerged over the last two years in the shape of a nineteen-year old Kenyan girl named Alice Toti, who had dominated the Grand Prix five thousand metre circuit and had run close to Beki's world record time.

They agreed on an approach consisting of six months of running ten miles a day at various speeds, mixed with sprint training and gym exercises. Beki would then go back home but continue her training and run in the major cross country events, followed by a return to Africa in the run up to the Olympics. She would run in a couple of Grand Prix events in order to get used to track running again.

And so began the next chapter of Beki's life. She rang Jamie every night and found that although she missed him terribly, it gave her momentum in the early days of the programme when her body was adjusting to the punishing regime. If she needed any more encouragement, Alice Toti broke the world five thousand metre record in the last Grand Prix event of the season.

Jamie was waiting for her at arrivals at Heathrow and she sprinted into his arms. He could not get over how much lighter she was and how firm her body had become. He whispered in her ear. 'Is regular sex permitted in your training programme?'

She smiled broadly at him and replied. 'It is but I don't know if you will be able to keep the new me satisfied!'

'There is only one way to find out.' he laughed.

They were invited to Polly's new house at the weekend for dinner. There had been major developments in her life over the last two years. She had decided after talking extensively with Stewart to invest the money she received from the Spanish Government in buying a racing stables and learning to become a trainer.

Stewart had invested money in the venture and the idea was that he would use his knowledge of the formbook to plan the horse's programmes as well as assisting Polly in the purchase of new horses.

She had gone on the British Horse Racing Authority's Trainer Course and had recently passed with flying colours. She and Stewart were set to go the Yearlings and Horses In Training Sales, with the objective of acquiring twenty-five horses. They had taken purchase orders from a number of friends including Chris and Selma and Jamie's parents.

Richard and Jessica agreed to become Assistant Trainer and travelling Head Lass respectively and were combining their duties with running their livery yard, while Jamie agreed to become stable jockey and to ride out when his other commitments permitted.

Both Sofia and Selma had become involved in the stables. Each looked after three horses and both of them learned to ride under Polly's expert tuition. However, Selma had to retire temporarily when she found herself pregnant again. She had again refused to check the sex of the child but

Chris's mother said that this one was definitely a boy, as Selma looked totally different from the way she did during her first pregnancy.

After a tour of the stables and the gallops, there were two major topics of conversation at dinner. The start of Polly's training career and the upcoming Olympics. The friends all marvelled at Beki's new appearance and it was decided that the women would fly out to Cape Town with Jamie for the ten thousand metres.

Beki said goodbye to Jamie with tears in her eyes as she left to travel to her training camp. The night before, while they were lying in bed, she told him that she would never leave him for a long period of time again and that she would like to have his baby when she returned home. He replied

'Let me get used to the idea, but more importantly, give me time to back our son or daughter to win an Olympic Gold medal within the next twenty years.'

'You never know' said Beki, 'He might turn out to be a show jumper!'

In the three months leading up to the Olympics, Beki ran in the Montreal and the Rome Grand Prix events. Alice Toti pointedly withdrew from both events. Beki won both races easily but her times were well outside world record schedule. Excitement mounted on the run up to Cape Town with the media describing the ten thousand metres as the race of the games. Both women said they were not into predictions and would let their running do the talking.

Taresh was concerned that there were four good Kenyans in the field, including Alice, and she felt that they would run tactically and try to disrupt Beki's rhythm, particularly if she ran from the front as usual. She and Beki did a lot of speed work, which they kept secret from the media and from her Kenyan opponents too.

In no time at all Beki was meeting Jamie and the girls at Cape Town airport on the eve of the race. She could feel Jamie running his eyes all over her and was glad that they were not staying together that night. They had a quick drink at the visitors' hotel and then Beki returned to the Olympic Village.

There was a buzz of anticipation in the capacity crowd as the runners lined up for the Olympic ten thousand metres final. This was what Beki had dreamed of most of her teenage and adult life. She could see Bela, Jamie, her family and the English women cheering loudly for her but she shut out that vision from her mind and focused on the next thirty minutes or so.

The gun fired and they started. The Kenyans went straight to the front and looked around continually during the first four laps as Beki tracked them easily in fifth position. After eight laps one of the Kenyans dropped back and was continually crowding Beki on the bends.

Beki soon had enough of this and moved up to take the lead in the tenth lap, although she had to run wide around the Kenyans to do so. She decided that she was not going to hang around and increased what was already a strong pace. With four laps left, she led Alice by three metres with an ever-widening gap of twenty metres to the rest of the field.

Things stayed the same until the bell rang for the final lap, amidst a huge roar from the crowd. Alice accelerated smoothly past Beki and went three metres ahead. This had never happened to Beki before but she dug in hard and when they came to the last bend, Alice had not increased her lead.

Beki called on reserves that she had never called on before and gradually inched closer. With ten metres left she pulled level, and the roar from the crowd became deafening. Both girls thrust themselves toward the line and crossed it together.

The wait for the result was agonising, with replay after replay taking place on the big screen. Could it be a dead heat for the first time ever in a distance race in the Olympics? The winner would also be a new world record holder, as the previous record had been smashed by three seconds!

The two protagonists had their arms around each other and were gasping their congratulations when the result came. Beki had won by one hundredth of a second. The finished print showed that her breast was the smallest fraction ahead of Alice as they burst the tape.

Beki was exhausted but she slowly made her way over to her supporters, who threw her the Ethiopian flag as she approached the barrier. She leaned over and threw her arms around Jamie's neck. Tears rolled down his cheeks as he whispered in her ear. 'I knew all that breast massage would pay off!'

Everyone else hugged her and Bela had a silver medal of her own. Not bad for two schoolmates from Hawassa.

Beki got her breath back in time for the medal ceremony and a host of media interviews in which she paid tribute to Alice who had pushed her to run faster than she had ever done before. Not normally given to emotional displays, Beki could not hold back the tears when she heard the Ethiopian National Anthem playing and the gold medal was placed around her neck.

The five thousand metres were due to take place in five days time, with two heats and then a final. Beki came to a decision in the interval.

Jamie was asleep in his room when he felt the covers slide back and a warm, firm body snuggled up to him. He woke up quickly when a hand gripped his manhood and slid it into a warm and wet vagina. He turned over to see Beki looking longingly at him. 'You cant do this darling. You have another race tomorrow.'

'My track racing days are over.' said Beki. 'I am going to retire undefeated. I have my gold medal now.'

'Are you sure Beki? The world will be expecting another epic race against Alice.'

'I have decided to retire undefeated. I used up all of my desire to win in that race. My times in training were nowhere near my previous world records. Allah granted me my greatest wish and now I want to start a new life.'

Taresh understood when Beki went to see her the following morning, as she could not believe how Beki had found the willpower to win the ten thousand metres. It turned out to be a wise decision as Alice destroyed the five thousand metre field, leading from the gun to win by thirty metres and

smashing her own world record in the process.

Five Years On

The Migrants syndicate were having lunch in the owners lounge while they waited for the big race in which their three year old, Son of Spartan, was due to race.

Stewart, Sofia, Poppy, Chris, Selma and Beki had clubbed together and bought two yearlings at the breeze-up sales two years earlier. Traveller had proved to be pretty ordinary, despite Poppy's well-documented training skills, which had taken her to sixth in the Trainers Table with an ever-expanding string of seventy-two horses.

However, Son of Spartan, a strapping grey colt, had proved a revelation. Cheaply bought at forty five thousand guineas, he had won both of his two-year old races, the first a seven furlong maiden race at Newbury where he made all of the running to win by an easy two lengths. This was not a surprise to Stewart who had been told by Jamie that he was the best two year old he had ever sat on and who took over one hundred thousand pounds out of the betting ring.

The colt then defied a rise in class to win the Group One Racing Post Two Year Old trophy at Doncaster in October, in a thrilling finish at odds of twelve to one, and spent the winter as third favourite for the first three year old classic, the two thousand Guineas.

Selma's two children were running around the dining room playing tag with Poppy's son and John. 'Be careful Hannah don't get Christopher too excited. His little legs can't keep up with you three!' said Selma.

Beki stooped to tuck her one-year-old baby daughter into her pushchair. She was already three months pregnant with a second child.

Selma stopped for a moment when she saw the children running around and thought about Marion and her family. She had been really distressed when she heard the news of their drowning and had determined to call her next female child Marion. It brought home to her how lucky she had been in rebuilding her life. Her family line would go on while Marion's whole family had disappeared off the face of the earth.

Poppy arrived at the table, her face flushed with excitement. 'Time to go to the paddock.' she announced and they all trooped out after her.

Spartan looked magnificent in the paddock as he walked around the perimeter, appearing to be totally relaxed, unlike two or three of his fourteen rivals who were on their toes and sweating.

They all listened closely as Poppy gave riding instructions to Jamie. 'Let's try to make the most of his stamina and determination. The favourite of Aiden O Brien's is not sure to stay the mile on breeding. Ride him in the first four and kick on as they go into the dip one and a half furlongs out.'

The runners all came over to the stands side during the race and Jamie followed Poppy's instructions to the letter. He urged his mount into the lead as they went into the dip. Spartan and the favourite, Russian Tsar, forged clear as they entered the final furlong. The favourite seemed to be travelling easily as he came up alongside the grey, however he simply could not get past as Spartan stuck his head out and battled all the way to the line, winning by a neck.

There was Euphoria at Newmarket with much hugging and kissing and a first classic winner for Polly and Jamie.

The following morning, thousands of miles away at lake Hawassa, an elderly man was seen to dance a jig after he read in the newspaper of Beki's success as a racehorse owner.

Nomads

If you have enjoyed Keith Sobey's first novel, which deals with the Migrant crisis, look out for his second, **Nomads** which tells the story of five male refugees and their bid for a better life.